UNDECORATE

UNDECORATE

THE NO-RULES APPROACH TO INTERIOR DESIGN

Christiane Lemieux

WITH RUMAAN ALAM

PHOTOGRAPHS BY MELANIE ACEVEDO

Clarkson Potter/Publishers
New York

Published in the United States by Clarkson Potter/Publishers, an imprint of
the Crown Publishing Group, a division of Random House, Inc., New York.
www.crownpublishing.com
www.clarksonpotter.com

CLARKSON POTTER is a trademark and POTTER with colophon is a
registered trademark of Random House, Inc.

Library of Congress Cataloging-in-Publication Data
Lemieux, Christiane.

 Undecorate / Christiane Lemieuxa and Rumaan Alam. —1st ed.
    p. cm.
 Includes index.
 1. Interior decoration. I. Alam, Rumaan. II. Title.

 NK2115.L434 2011
 747—dc22

                         2010034342

ISBN 978-0-307-46315-9

Printed in China

Book and jacket design by Amy Sly

10 9 8 7 6 5 4 3

First Edition

TO
JOSHUA
AND
JENNA

CONTENTS

The Decorators Without Borders
17

The Career Opportunists
59

The Incurable Collectors
89

The Imperfectionists
127

The Self-Starters
171

The Environmentalists
217

FOREWORD

a few years back, a jewelry designer friend of mine hired one of the country's top decorators—a man high on my own if-money-were-no-object short list—to do up her apartment. He spent six months hunting for clean-lined twentieth-century antiques by the likes of Poul Kjaerholm and Tommi Parzinger. He treated the walls with pewter-leaf, stuffed furniture with horsehair, and created custom pieces, such as a fabulously long, silk-velvet sofa. The result was breathtaking: tailored and elegant and undeniably glamorous. It was perfect—only for someone else's life.

This friend of mine is a wonderfully exuberant, colorful, chic, and witty woman who modestly manages a thriving business with a couple of lively children underfoot. The tonally restrained and rather formal apartment the decorator created for her seemed to demand a different sort of occupant—someone more conventional and reserved, with the sort of children who might be summoned from their playroom to kiss mummy goodnight and then ushered out again. Eventually, she couldn't take it anymore and moved to a new apartment nearby. There she made a home in her own image: one that was exuberant, full of color, chic, and witty—and much more casual.

The norm used to be that lives conformed largely to the dictates of the house, rather than the other way around. Those were the dark ages of decorating, before the rise of the Internet and accessible good design. It's hard to remember now, but even a decade ago there weren't any shelter magazines or blogs trafficking in the home-grown style of the passionate amateur. We once viewed mostly pristinely decorated homes across the chasm of perfectly styled magazine photographs—that often revealed, if unintentionally, the homes' lack of personality. In our new, democratized world, anyone with his or her own sense of style and a clever knack for pulling things together can reach and inspire us.

This doesn't mean that everything that bubbles up on the Web is worth taking note of. But wading through a bit of mediocrity is a small price to pay for the profusion of original talent, fresh energy, and, often, unconventional ideas that can readily be found. Christiane Lemiuex has created a design book culled from the best of this indigenous revolution: a collection of homes that exemplifies the diversity of style happening now. What she calls 'undecorating' is a movement blissfully free of any ideological stance. Here you will find no preaching on the moral superiority of modernism, or hewing to the hegemony of classical interior design. If there is any devotion to a single period or school of design, it is personal and heartfelt.

This is decorating that is passionate *and* particular. Each of the homes featured could *only* be the home of the person who made it, so much does each reflect and enhance the individual lives it contains. (If you try to envision the sophisticated Francophile on pages 32–43 in the vintage fantasyland featured on pages 78–87, or the auto fanatics profiled on pages 102–111 in the pared-back elegance on pages 204–215, it simply wouldn't make sense.) In any of these homes you could very well find handmade art, delicious dinners, domestic spats, lazy afternoons, bad days, wonderful parties, financial struggles, or broken dishwashers. In these pages, real life shows itself to be the muse of good design.

The experience that Christiane has created feels less like a conventional decorating book and more like a round robin of visits with friends. I was lucky enough to get to know several of the people featured in the book—including Christiane herself—in the four years (2005–2009) I was editor of *Domino* magazine. The author is precisely the kind of original talent we loved to feature. As a designer of textiles and bedding, Christiane brings her great style into many homes. And she has created a home for her family that channels who they are and the kind of life she wants to make for them.

At *Domino,* when we were on the fence about whether to photograph a house for our pages, we would ask ourselves if it seemed like it would be a fun place to be invited over for a drink. Oftentimes, an interior might be tasteful and well-executed, but it seemed to lack a crucial *something.* Just like my jewelry designer friend's place, which while gorgeous, didn't feel exciting or inviting. That ineffable something is vibrancy and energy—or you might call it love, or quirk, or personality. However you define it, *Undecorate* is chock full of it. And no home should be without it.

—Deborah Needleman

INTRODUCTION

i n service of what I do for a living, I get to indulge in a lot of things that only barely count as work. I get to peruse flea markets and out-of-the-way vintage shops, to study how the pros of yesteryear practiced their arts. I get to watch movies and take mental notes on the sets and costumes, and I get to stop by the fancy boutiques and stay abreast of what's going on in the world of fashion. (At least that's what I tell myself.) I get to buy as many magazines and books as I can carry, because I never know where I'm going to spot the thing that sparks my interest.

It's not a bad life.

Since I founded DwellStudio in 2000, however, the thing that's had probably the biggest impact on me, creatively and professionally, has been the Internet. It's no exaggeration that the Internet has totally changed the way the world works. It used to be that you'd design something (anything: a dress, a pillow, a car) and then send it out into the world, and the only way to gauge its success would be to look at how many people bought it. But with the proliferation of design websites and personal blogs, a whole new window has opened up: I get to see how people are actually living, whether it's with the bedding, tabletop, and home accessories we design at DwellStudio or with the stuff they've turned up while trolling eBay. I used to turn to the experts—the fashion and interior designers of the world. These days, I much prefer to go to the amateurs. The Internet offers so much proof that the most vibrant style ideas are coming from the minds of real people.

It was not always so. Less than a generation ago, the ultimate expression of taste was to hire a big-name decorator to put his or her own stamp on your home. The expert would deliver everything from silk-upholstered ceilings to the sugar bowl on the kitchen counter, and you had only to move in and enjoy the bragging rights.

I still love that traditional decorator-as-artiste design book. I always pore over whatever the season has to offer—to see how one singular talent has worked his or her magic in stately homes all across the world. It's the stuff of pure fantasy: mansions in East Hampton and Aspen, Lake Como and La Jolla; tables laid with Dresden china; powder rooms clad in hand-painted wallpaper; tufted leather sofas as long as limousines. It is also instructive to see how one designer consistently

uses a certain color palette or references a particular historical moment. These books offer a focused, detailed look at one personality, one point of view.

But what makes for a great coffee table book doesn't necessarily make much sense for real life. Most real people don't hire a decorator and then expect to move into a flawlessly furnished house six months later. The most stylish people these days understand this fundamental aspect of good living: it's always evolving. Great style isn't necessarily a finished product so much as it is an ongoing process.

When I decided to write a book of my own, I knew I wanted it to be about people who understand this contradiction. I wanted it to capture the dazzling variety—the many different ways of living—that I so love about the Internet. I wanted it to be about the multiplicity of styles that are flourishing out there right now, with or without the stamp of approval of some trained professional. I wanted to write a book about the kinds of people who catch my eye, time and again—a book about real people, and real style. It's true that most of the people you'll meet in these pages have some kind of relationship (usually a working one) to the worlds of art and design and fashion. But their homes feel so authentic, so achievable. These aren't flawless residences straight from the pages of some interiors magazine; these homes are imperfect and unbuttoned, a lesson in how to live whether you're a fashion designer or a dentist.

The variety of styles I see on the Internet doesn't necessarily translate seamlessly to book form. Or so the editors kept telling me. We needed to narrow it down a little, to sift through all the great design and inspired ideas that are out there and figure out what it all meant. So I spent months looking at everything from slick, well-designed blogs to humble sites documenting one homeowner's DIY renovation. And somewhere along the way I heard a word that stuck in my head, a word that seemed to me to encapsulate the one common thread in all these great spaces. Because design has its rules, and what I was noticing more and more is that the most stylish people are willing to disregard those rules. And this word I picked up from who-knows-where seems a very apt one for this approach to decorating. That word is *undecorated.*

What does it mean to undecorate? A fine question.

It's mixing fine antiques with your collection of Cher Barbie dolls, as Harry Heissmann does in his description-defying apartment in Brooklyn Heights. It's leaving temporary party decorations up for years because they just somehow seem right, as Erica Tanov does in her ridiculously beautiful California house. It's wedging antique columns into a suburban house, or parking your cars in the living room, or building your own altar, or hanging vintage advertising posters in your toddler's bedroom. Undecorated is following your instinct, even when it's telling you to do something a little crazy, a little different, something against the rules.

The homes featured in these pages reflect their owners' fearless approach to style. An approach that has nothing to do with trends (though inside you'll find all the trends that are current now or ever have been, done pretty terrifically), and it has nothing to do with the rules. So you can have a period dining room adjacent to your modern kitchen, if that's what you want, or a pink accent wall, or wallpaper on the ceiling. Stranger things have been done, and have still looked plenty chic. Undecorating isn't haphazard style; it's not thought-free. It's about being guided by something other than the traditional constraints—whether it's your commitment to the environment, or your love of polka dots, or the fact that you want to feel like you're in Paris when you live in Peoria.

OPPOSITE LEFT In Erica Tanov's home, even everyday essentials like pencils are displayed with flair. OPPOSITE RIGHT Harry Heissmann's Brooklyn home is devoted to collections—even humble ones, like cans of Campbell's soup with Warhol-inspired labels. PREVIOUS PAGE In their Tennessee abode, Genifer Goodman Sohr and Benjamin Sohr have created what seems like an oxymoron: a modern log cabin home.

If you undecorate, you acknowledge that life is a fluid thing, and accordingly, that style is a flexible thing. Undecorated style isn't one wholesale thing—it's a shifting target, and has much more to do with process than with finished product. It's decorating not to meet the specifications set down by some professional, or to fulfill the requirements of some expert, but to meet your own needs, whatever you decide those are. It's about putting your philosophy first, putting your personality first, and letting your signature style blossom naturally from the decisions you make.

The undecorated style is as all-encompassing and wide-ranging as the country in which it was born. It's Kim Ficaro and James Wilson's serene walk-up railroad apartment in New York City and Caitlin Wylde's bric-a-brac-strewn home in Los Angeles, and everything in between. I think of this book as itself an exercise in undecorated style. It's unlike most big, fancy design books. Yes, it's full of gorgeous pictures (courtesy of our photographer, Melanie Acevedo), but our ragtag crew—Melanie, her assistants, my colleague Molly Peterson, and I—rolled up to all the houses featured in these pages without a stylist or a hair and makeup person to tweak our subjects' looks. What you're seeing is how people actually live, amid baby toys, curious pets, and daily household clutter. Most houses would not hold up to this kind of warts-and-all examination, but what we've put together here is a peek into the homes of some very audacious, stylish people. This isn't that perfect book of flawless interiors you're used to (and which, I confess, I still love); it is something more cutting-edge, more documentary-like—a look at how people are really living right now—and a snapshot of the beginning of a movement.

Because that's what undecorating is, I think, in its own humble way: a movement. From the moment I first heard it, *undecorate* as a word has stuck with me, a small word carrying a big answer to the establishment way of thinking. It's not about heirlooms, so it's easy on the wallet. It's not about store-bought perfection, so it's easy on the planet. It's about being unafraid to do things yourself (something else the Internet has made so easy; in this day and age you can learn almost anything online). It's about prioritizing ease over elegance, good vibes over grandiosity. It's about not letting the little imperfections of the daily grind get in the way of your having a chic lifestyle. Unsure how to accomplish these things? It's no matter. Undecorate is an easygoing philosophy, and this book is full of ideas— ideas I invite you to steal. To achieve a true undecorated style you don't need custom furniture or a name-brand architect. You don't need much more than an open mind. The people whom I met and learned from, the people you're about to meet, prove that handily. They've perfected American style, something I'd always assumed was indefinable. Here it is: unafraid, unabashed, unfussy—and undecorated. Enjoy.

In Christina Sacalis's New Jersey house, everything from walls to tables to a well-loved pair of chairs has the charming patina of age and everyday use—because sometimes nothing is more stylish than a little wear and tear.

THE DECORATORS WITHOUT BORDERS

When you're decorating, you shouldn't be bound by anything more than your imagination. Decorating pros are schooled, and will always work with some awareness of the rules. What these three homes have in common is their audacious disregard for the rules. It's not just that their owners have broken a few widely held dicta; what makes these homes quintessentially undecorated isn't that there are snapshots hanging in the dining room, or windows without curtains. The one thing every decorator must grapple with is context. A home is, after all, defined by the place where it is located—or so you might think. These three homes brilliantly show that it is possible to transcend even geography to create the space you want.

Andy Newcom's gracious living room

THINK OF ENGLAND

**LISA BORGNES GIRAMONTI AND PIERO GIRAMONTI,
LOS ANGELES, CALIFORNIA**

Hollywood will always be a city of dreams, a place where life is what
you make it, a city where even a proper English manor house fits
in beautifully.

In the American West, bigger is better. That's truer perhaps nowhere than in
Los Angeles—a company town where the Hollywood ethos holds that the
key to happiness is, frankly, more. Accordingly, for their first eighteen months in
California, transplanted New Yorkers Lisa Borgnes Giramonti, Piero Giramonti,
and their son, Luca, lived as the natives do: in a too-big, too-grand house. But on
one of the family's frequent trips, this one to India, Lisa had an awakening of
sorts: it was time to simplify. "We were living in a Hummer," she says, "and I
wanted to live in a Prius."

So the family moved, to a much smaller and humbler Monterey colonial in
Hollywood, a blank canvas upon which Lisa, an artist and a prolific design blogger,
could create a home to suit the modest needs of her family of three. "Inside, the
house was nothing more than a white box—I could really put my imprint on it,"
she explains. She immediately set out to reference her upbringing abroad as her
touchstone throughout the process. "I've always had a reverence for England," Lisa
says. "I lived there as a child, and had a very enchanted time there."

Lisa jokingly refers to the finished house as Lilliput Manor. It's an apt name,
perfectly capturing the home's alluring contradiction—it's smaller, sure, and it's in
California, but it is very much an English manor house, charmingly and eccentri-
cally updated for modern life.

A sense of play and fun runs throughout
the home's rooms, and this begins the moment
a guest enters the house, via the carved brass

"I wanted the room to feel grand," says Lisa. The window
cornices help accomplish that goal nicely; their grandeur is
tempered by the neutral Peter Dunham fabric. The Union
Jack pillow on the daybed is a clear acknowledgment of
Lisa's Anglophilia.

In days gone by,
a work like mine
Would have admirers
all in line.
No more are home arts
prized like rubies,
Today we must have
perky boobies.

LISA BORGNES 2000
LOS ANGELES A.D.

bird door knocker, purchased from a roadside vendor in rural India. It's a whimsical touch—a reminder that this is to be one woman's modern-day interpretation of a classic English home—and the first of many beloved souvenirs with which the well-traveled Giramontis have furnished their house. Inside the foyer, one is transported from the former colonies directly to England as lavishly patterned wallpaper from Clarence House, virtually embraces visitors. The botanic print has a timeless quality; a little something straight out of Jane Austen—but it's offset by a decidedly non-English ikat-upholstered bench.

This interplay between old England and the New World continues in the adjacent dining room. It's a small space, so rather than aim for a grand, formal room, Lisa decided to keep things simple and cozy. "I wanted it to feel like you were in an English pub on a Sunday afternoon," she says. The trompe l'oeil hand-printed bookcase wallpaper by English designer Deborah Bowness lends the room an aura of laid-back comfort—you can almost smell the worn leather of all those well-thumbed volumes. It's

ABOVE LEFT The brass knocker is one of many souvenirs the well-traveled family has incorporated into their home. **ABOVE RIGHT** "I was so excited when we found this house," says Lisa. "A little Monterey Colonial, perfectly preserved outside—and inside a white box, so I could really put my imprint on it." **OPPOSITE** The bench's upholstery was repurposed from an online discovery. "Ikat is so expensive—instead of buying fabric, I just found this Uzbek robe on eBay," says Lisa.

a quirky but still sophisticated statement: wallpaper as fine art.

To complement the faux library, Lisa chose an eclectic mix of furnishings with a similarly broken-in feel: an inherited midcentury Danish dining table paired with a bench fashioned from horseshoes, a forties-era relic discovered in a London flea market that dates from a time when designers had to contend with the widespread rationing of raw materials. Hanging on the far wall is an assortment of photos from Lisa's travels. "There's a famous dictum that says never put personal photos in your dining room," she acknowledges. "I broke the rule. I always want to be surrounded by friends and places and things I cherish." It's an unusual choice—more suited, some might say, to a breakfast nook than a proper dining room—but it has the desired effect. Even a first-time visitor can't help but feel at home here.

Guests pass through the dining room into a hallway that opens to the serene living room, which serves many functions, not the least of which is to showcase Lisa's artwork. Her chosen medium is embroidery, and her oversize samplers are a strikingly contemporary foil to the room's velvet upholstered chairs and dramatic window cornices. "I call these postmodern samplers," Lisa explains. "In the 1700s, this work documented women's lives, or was a sociological record of how people lived." In her idiosyn-

ABOVE AND BELOW In the living room, some of Lisa and Piero's accumulated treasures and favorite books are on display alongside two of Lisa's embroidered pieces: a dinner scene and the interior of her old New York City apartment. **OPPOSITE** The upholstered swing door (a standard-issue partition wrapped in vinyl) recalls splendid manor houses, with their strict division of the upstairs and downstairs sets.

cratic take, the classic form is turned on its head with acerbically modern text. Lisa also embroiders scenes, working from favorite snapshots; one such work on display, capturing a beloved former apartment, speaks to the artist's long-standing interest in interiors.

The living room walls and ceiling are painted slightly different shades of blue, so the color of the space changes depending on how the light falls at a given time of day. It's a subtle choice meant to bring to life the still lifes and the myriad vignettes showcasing the family's many souvenirs, artworks, cherished books, and impossible-to-classify objets. The treasures on display recall grand halls where oversize oils are hung, salon style, one atop the other. The effect is dazzling—a visual bounty that's meant to tell guests the story of the family members' lives. Some people might shrink from putting so many things on display, but Lisa has been liberated by the comparatively small confines of this house. "Because the rooms are smaller, I could really let loose," she explains. Small spaces require less wallpaper and paint, fewer light fixtures and furnishings, which

ABOVE "I wanted to have a lot of seating areas," says Lisa. "I love how the daybed bridges both areas of the living room. It makes the room feel so welcoming." OPPOSITE: ABOVE LEFT AND BELOW RIGHT When artfully arranged, clutter feels downright chic. ABOVE RIGHT One of Lisa's samplers is on display in the living room—fittingly, as both her art and her décor balance the traditional and the modern. BELOW LEFT More of Lisa's handiwork.

makes filling them with quality pieces much easier on the wallet.

"I'm not much of a sun person," Lisa says, laughing. To counter the brilliant LA sunshine and the fact that so much of life in this part of the country takes place out of doors, she painted her upstairs office an unexpectedly subdued hue. Muted but not dark, the room's palette helps to turn its occupant's attention inward—only appropriate for a study. Here as elsewhere the mix of decorative elements is eclectic, a reflection of the inhabitant's varied interests. While the lines of the long couch and the modern desk are clean and simple, the tattered rug (cleverly set atop a modern sisal for contrast) and the huge landscape by American painter Ernest Leonard Blumenschein balance out those classically midcentury silhouettes. In contrast to the downstairs living room, the décor here is restrained; this is a room where Lisa can focus. She couldn't, however, tame altogether her instinct to gather and display, as evidenced by her ever-evolving and overcrowded inspiration bulletin board.

One of the things Lisa had hoped for in relocating was a home where her family would be physically—and, in turn, emotionally—closer to one another. (Again, she calls the place Lilliput Manor for a reason.) Still, though the office, the master bedroom, and Luca's room are physically close, stylistically each occupies its own world.

ABOVE Dark walls are a surprising choice in the sun-splashed office, but they work nicely—especially when balanced by the light furniture. BELOW Lisa and her son, Luca. OPPOSITE The desk chair is clad in the same fabric as a chair in the downstairs living room. "Stripes go with everything," Lisa declares. The crowded inspiration board is evidence of a true polymath; in addition to working as an artist, Lisa is a dedicated blogger, writing about style and whatever else inspires her at A Bloomsbury Life.

Lisa aimed to make the master bedroom feel like a guest suite in an English manor house. The subtle pitch of the ceiling creates the impression that you're up in the eaves of some sprawling country house (Gosford Park, perhaps), a guest for a weekend of foxhunting. If indeed this were a room in such a manse, it would have a name—how else to differentiate when you've got forty spare bedrooms?—and no doubt it would be called the Crest Room. The dominant decorative motif here is the heavy wooden crests Lisa has hung directly over the bed. "They're antique heraldic crests from Toledo, Spain," she says. She loves their continental, noble appeal. Here, they establish a sense of symmetry and formality (continued in the matching lamps and mirrored nightstands). They're a grandiose gesture and, as such, a little risky, but Lisa has balanced these big accessories with some casual, inviting Indian textiles and modern pillows.

Luca's room is decorated as thoughtfully as any other space in the house, with a lightness of touch that's suited to a child's room—though the results are chic rather than baby-ish. In large part that's due to the fact that

ABOVE Symmetry is always in style—in the master bedroom, everything (nightstands, pillows, lamps, the crests over the bed) is paired up, giving the space a serene and balanced feel. **OPPOSITE** Lisa's envy-inducing walk-in closet is functional more than anything, but she's decorated it with personal touches, like the traditional Dala horse, a nod to her father's Scandinavian heritage.

instead of purchasing a lot of kid-size furniture he'd eventually outgrow, Mom and Dad decided to furnish their son's space with pieces already in their collection. The century-old Italian bed was once their master bed; the tall Arne Jacobsen desk chair is one of a set of ten deemed too imposing for the new, small dining room. Bright flourishes, such as the dyed red hide rugs and a selection of work by their burgeoning young artist, add an appropriately youthful whimsy to the room. "I wanted to give my son a sense of magic and innocence," Lisa says.

Throughout the house, it's the details that are most telling, from the upholstered door in the dining room to the Union Jack pillow in the living room, from the repetition of motifs (Indian fabrics, the blue-and-gray palette) to the tiny pineapple finials on the stair rods. "In the eighteenth century, retired sea captains would put pineapples on their homes to signal a safe return home," explains Lisa. "That's how we feel here. We're not moving anymore. We're home for good."

There's no need to buy furniture specifically designed for kids—they'll only outgrow it eventually anyway. Luca's room is filled with sophisticated pieces handed down from Mom and Dad.

SPLENDOR IN THE GRASS

ANDY NEWCOM, KANSAS CITY, KANSAS

With do-it-yourself ingenuity, a tendency to think as big as possible, and a truly expert team, one man has created a home that's not bound by its suburban lot.

I f our homes express our personalities, moving affords us a singular opportunity: to change. "I lived in my last house for fifteen years," says Andy Newcom. "That house was about two thousand square feet, and I didn't need that much space. This was all about simplifying. It was time to reinvent myself."

It's a telling statement: for Andy, the line between himself and his home is a nebulous one. The house is his creative outlet, and in creating a home for himself he bravely disregarded rules and received wisdom to forge from an otherwise unassuming suburban cottage a showpiece. The house is full of baronial flourishes, yet is still somehow humble. It's sophisticated yet down-to-earth. It's home as a pure expression of its inhabitant, and it's not bound by the rules of geography or, frankly, logic. You leave Kansas City at the door and enter a whole new world.

"This house was built in the early 1940s," Andy says. "It's a little two-bedroom home that was your typical grandma house. It didn't have tons of character, but I immediately loved it." Some of the most important decisions one makes (from what house to buy to what color to paint the powder room) are intuitive. Perhaps it's just a matter of chemistry, as in a romance, or perhaps Andy sensed something in the modest home that others might not have: potential. Most likely, it was a combination of the two. Nevertheless, he embarked on the process of making the house his own.

Andy is quick to point out that he didn't do it alone. He worked closely with his parents, now both in their eighties, on virtually every aspect of the home's renovation and decoration. He credits them both for his

Though the living room feels rooted in the past, it's all an illusion. "There's no original architecture inside," confesses Andy. The graceful moldings on the wall and at the ceiling add texture and a sense of history to the space—a chic juxtaposition to the modern furniture.

On the stack of books:

Seasonal Home
DECOR   SO CHIC
1000 GARDEN IDEAS
FRENCH HOME   Josephine Ryan
Sensual living   CLAIRE LLOYD

own artistic eye, and feels he's inherited some of his father's do-it-yourself spirit. The process of working on this home together was more than just a simple renovation; it was Andy's way of acknowledging his parents' profound influence on his aesthetic and his life.

Andy was uniquely equipped to tackle a home's transformation. Not only did he have his parents' accrued decades of insight and experience, but he himself had spent a lifetime collecting and honing his eye. The home's interior was carefully designed to show to best advantage the many impressive antiques and collectibles he's amassed. They're not simply collections, though—they're pieces he actually lives with. The close collaboration and his personal attachment to his many furnishings and decorative objects contribute to the sense that the home isn't exactly in Kansas City—or in this century, for that matter. Andy has a way of decorating with antiques that isn't precious or lofty; he lives the way people once did: in another, more genteel time. It's a fantasy, to be sure, so it's not without its appeal.

ABOVE LEFT Andy with his parents, Barney and Jean Newcom. He and his father laid the herringbone brick floor themselves. ABOVE RIGHT Weathered furniture, chipped bowls, and well-read books give the sunroom a comfortably lived-in feel. OPPOSITE Andy transformed a screened-in porch into a full-on sunroom. The concrete bunnies are a whimsical rejoinder to the classical bust. "I'm very selective about the artwork, because I don't have a lot of wall space," says Andy. "But statuary is great because you can just plop it anywhere."

The house's simple façade doesn't prepare one for the grand architectural touches within. For example, the stunning wood columns topped with intricately carved plaster capitals that separate the living room from the dining room. The addition of such details contributes to the fantasy that, instead of a modern-day Kansas City suburban home, guests have entered a London town house or a Parisian pied-à-terre. Inside the dining room, Andy and his father added crown moldings and a chair rail, the latter constructed to create the illusion that the massive sideboard is in fact built-in. "Dad is really brilliant," Andy says, in awe. "He can make anything."

This sleight of hand with the sideboard, and the oversize mirror above it, helps create the impression that the tiny room is bigger than it is. Despite the intimate proportions, Andy hasn't shied away from making grand statements. "I have a flair for the dramatic," he admits. That's something of an understatement. The 1930s table base is topped with marble and surrounded by a sextet of antique Venetian-style chairs. On the sideboard is a pair of his many statues, depicting two of the four seasons. "Most people keep statuary outside," Andy acknowledges, laughing. "I happen to love anything that weighs over five hundred pounds." It's perhaps counterintuitive, but there's a lesson here. Rather than try to fool you into thinking the room is bigger than it is, Andy has simply used every available inch of space. The result is a room that somehow perfectly balances comfort and splendor.

In the dining room, Andy uses tried and true tricks, like filling the tiny room with big furniture and aligning mirrors and lighting, to create the illusion of space.

Despite the preponderance of antiques, Andy isn't averse to modern design touches. There's the pendant lamp overhead and the decidedly more contemporary adjacent living room. "I don't care where things are from," he explains. "I just want the right look." To achieve that in the living room, he paired the cream Naugahyde-clad antique sofa with a duo of tufted leather armchairs in a brilliant red. It's an eye-catching shade in any context, and in the otherwise subdued home, the color fairly glows. The simple marble-topped occasional tables from CB2 are another unexpectedly modern flourish—though, of course, they're offset by the grand French demi-ture console table nearby. (It once stood inside an opera house.) The elements in the room seesaw thus; the undulating lines of the grandfather clock in the corner have a modern counterpoint in the streamlined torchiere between the armchairs. Livable rooms are all about this unique balance. Too many antiques and the space would feel like a museum—stunning, but ultimately standoffish. The modern touches are the corrective to that; the dining table might seem fit for a king, but anyone can imagine curling up in those armchairs.

Perhaps the most successful juxtaposition in this room, though, is found in Andy's use of contemporary art. It's testament to his wide-ranging tastes that the same man who stalks salvage yards in search of pristine columns is also attracted to modern paintings. Because he's filled the house only with things he genuinely loves, though, the unlikely mix somehow works. The art—a

ABOVE Glass and white accents fade nicely into the background, keeping visual clutter at a minimum. **BELOW** The painting is actually part of a triptych; Andy hung the series' other two canvases on a nearby wall. **OPPOSITE** Modern furniture—the bright red chairs, the simple pair of tables—balance out the room's more fanciful touches.

triptych by Kansas City painter Tom Gregg, a mosaic that Andy commissioned from friend and colleague Donna Van Hooser—contrasts nicely with the room's elaborate trim work.

Though he was well equipped to tackle most of the house's renovation himself, there were certain details Andy was dead set on, and for these he needed to call in the specialists. "I can be stubborn about things," he says, with a laugh. He was determined to replace the existing window with the oversize oval-shaped one, and preferred the antique cast-iron sink to the existing fixture. It was sheer good fortune that the two happened to fit together perfectly in the modest kitchen, and these old-world flourishes that are in keeping with the tone Andy established in the dining room do make the space feel more sophisticated. The graphic fabric skirt underneath the wide sink lends a bit of softness and texture to the room, which is admittedly not the most functional space. (Andy demurs that he's not much of a cook.) Instead of foodstuffs or appliances, he's used the open shelving to

ABOVE LEFT "I love the look of ironstone," Andy says of his collection of china. "The forms are so simple and beautiful—some of the pieces feel contemporary." **ABOVE RIGHT** "I had a minimal budget but I really wanted beams in the ceiling," Andy says. "My builder had the great idea to use split rail posts. It's exactly the look I wanted." **OPPOSITE** "When you paint the walls and the floor white, you have no horizon line," Andy says. "Things almost seem to float." Thus big pieces like the vintage school table and the giant cast iron urns don't overwhelm the all-white studio.

display highlights from his extensive collection of English ironstone china.

The other big job that required professional intervention was raising the roof. "When I bought this house I certainly had no intention of taking the roof off," Andy says. But he is a man who knows what he wants. In need of a bit more space, he was faced with the dilemma of building up or out. He decided in favor of the former, to preserve the home's original, modest footprint—the better to retain the cottage charm that had attracted him to the house in the first place. This big move allowed Andy to create a second-story garret that's straight out of *La Bohème*.

The upstairs studio was a significant addition, one that Newcom fought hard for. "A couple of the contractors didn't want to do such a steep pitch on the roof," he recalls. "But I wanted the charm. I wanted a little bit of drama. I wanted a wow factor." He has more than achieved that—the study is pure fantasy come to life, the kind of room one imagines some old master might have inhabited. It's an elegant but private space; the pieces lovingly on display are there simply for their owner's enjoyment. This room—really, the whole house—is a reminder that our homes need to reflect us.

ABOVE In the garret, as elsewhere, artworks abound. **BELOW** Old books, weathered boxes, and a bird's nest add a little charm to Andy's workspace. **OPPOSITE** A stack of art books; a painting leaned casually against the wall—disarray can be so stylish.

PIECED TOGETHER

GENIFER GOODMAN SOHR AND BENJAMIN SOHR, NASHVILLE, TENNESSEE

A duo of reformed nomads have created the home they've always dreamt of inside an architectural anomaly that's both out of place and out of time.

after years of juggling corporate careers involving near-constant travel, Genifer Goodman Sohr and Benjamin Sohr decided it was time for a life change. The couple, who had been living in San Francisco, packed up and moved to Benjamin's native Nashville, to be closer to his family, settle down, and buy a house. To most young professionals on the coasts, Tennessee conjures images of the over-the-top mansions of music royalty (Graceland, anyone?) or that unfortunate modern blight, the McMansion. But the place the Sohrs now call home is a world away from those of its neighbors in Nashville: a quirky architectural assemblage that's stunning inside and out, and emblematic of just how far a creative spirit and a willingness to ignore pesky realities such as geography can take you.

"The house kind of found us," Genifer says, laughing. "There was a particular street Benjamin had always loved, and one day we were just driving around and we saw this place and thought, 'That could be interesting.'" That descriptor doesn't quite do justice to this particular house: the structure is comprised of several different log cabins that date back to the early 1800s. They were brought here from various sites in Kentucky and assembled into one home in the 1950s. "No one had lived here for a long time, and it was untouched," Genifer recalls. "We decided that we could make it work."

When decorating, one can always go the safe route, coordinating interior style to architectural style. But when dealing with a home as idiosyncratic as this, there's no rule book to consult. Who in this day and age knows how to decorate a log cabin? So rather than aim for authenticity, Genifer and Benjamin decided to decorate by instinct, filling the home with pieces they love, creating workable spaces for a family of four, and assuming that somehow it would all come together in the end—as it has.

The long kitchen island was inspired by the years both Genifer and Benjamin spent living out of hotels—and dining at hotel bars. There's ample space for family and guests to congregate, whether it's for a meal, to help with the cooking, or just to hang out.

The vivid poppy-red front door that welcomes guests provides a bold contrast to the home's woody exterior. "The door is original; the color makes the house feel updated and contemporary," Genifer says. This one exterior detail signals what lies inside: a blend of that quintessential log cabin-ness with a bright modern sensibility. It's especially instructive to begin a tour of this house at that front door. "We used the door's red as an accent color throughout the house," Genifer explains. Little pops of red (the ice bucket on the bar, the box on the coffee table) are a subtle touch throughout the main living areas, precisely the kind of easily overlooked detail that adds another layer of polish to a home. Red is by no means the dominant color, though; that would be white. It's on the banisters and railings, and shows up on lampshades, vessels, even the andirons in the fireplaces. "We didn't touch the log walls, of course," Genifer says, "but we did add some drywall, as a relief from all that wood." By adding crisp whites for contrast and eschewing window coverings in favor of unfettered light, Genifer and Benjamin managed to create what should be a contradiction in terms: a light-filled wood cabin.

ABOVE The family homestead was pieced together from several old log cabins. **OPPOSITE** Throughout the house, white walls and trim and little bits of bright color balance out the wooden floors, walls, and overhead beams.

Decorating can be one of those tricky issues in a relationship, one not addressed by most therapists. That was certainly the case with this family. "Benjamin has a super modern aesthetic," says Genifer, "and I'm more eclectic and feminine." Of course, as with so many other issues, compromise was key. The sofa represents a happy medium between the couple's disparate tastes: it's a modern Italian design clad in a toile slipcover made by Genifer's mother. The juxtaposition of the sleek lines and comparatively ornate textiles is playful and unexpected, and the result is more than just a sofa both of them can live with—it's a chic and totally original statement, and the star attraction in the room.

The main living room has two separate seating areas, though the aim wasn't to have one formal zone in contrast to a comfier spot. The layout is simply a function of the room's proportions and the couple's impressive collection of interesting furniture and objects, the bulk of them flea market finds. Both sections of the living room are dominated by pairs—

ABOVE LEFT The family abandoned the conventional wisdom, using a white rug in a household with kids. Red accents are a connective thread throughout the rooms. **ABOVE RIGHT** "I love a bargain," says Genifer. "I love thrift stores—I love finding unexpected things that no one else wanted." She found the bird embroidery in a junk store. **OPPOSITE** Emeco's iconic aluminum chairs are a modern touch in the dining room, contrasting nicely with the wooden walls, floor, and ceiling. "I wanted to get as much light as possible," says Genifer. "So instead of curtains, I just used a tension rod with a bit of fabric. It's a simple idea I stole from my mom."

on the far end, the framed pieces over the fireplace; in the center of the room, the two brown leather sofas. Thus, both zones of the room have an element of symmetry that helps further define and distinguish them from each other. Both the art and the sofas are vintage (from markets in Miami and San Francisco, respectively), and though they're undeniably special, Genifer avoids treating anything in the house with any undue reverence. "Those sofas are a great scale," she says. "But most important, they're durable. The kids cannot destroy them."

There are two kids in residence, Lucy and Oden, and though the grown-ups have clearly put significant effort into making the home beautiful, they have an easygoing attitude toward their stuff. "Things may be vintage, but we don't worry if they get knocked around," Genifer says. "The painters thought we were crazy for doing white walls because we have kids, but we don't stress about things being ruined." This laid-back approach allows the family to actually live with and enjoy the many things they've amassed—something all too easily overlooked when decorating.

Mom and Dad didn't even bother with kiddie furniture: the younger residents have rooms as sophisticated as (but more playful than) any other in the home. In Lucy's room, as in the living room, liberal doses of white help counter the very present log walls. The star attraction is quite naturally the bed. "That was the first piece of furniture I ever bought," Genifer recalls. "When I was eighteen I bought it at an estate sale." The simple finish

From the abstract art above the fireplace to the midcentury Bertoia chairs to the elaborate toile of the sofa, the living room is a hodgepodge of styles, but by keeping the arrangement of furniture and objects orderly and balanced, the overall feeling is one of cohesion—even calm.

the ceilings are high, so the room is small in scale but not claustrophobic."

Additions and renovated rooms can often feel disconnected from the main body of a house, but careful decorative touches can help unify new and old spaces. Here, the gray palette picks up on the house's exterior color scheme, while overhead, nonstructural beams help the bedroom feel architecturally related to the rest of the house.

The only other big structural intervention Genifer and Benjamin undertook before moving in was to transform the small galley into a massive and impressive kitchen that's the home's true heart. High ceilings, clean white walls, and generous windows bring as much light as possible into the soaring space. The fireplace, original to the house, gives the new modern kitchen an old-fashioned anchor (but it's no longer used for cooking as once it was). "We always knew if we ever had the space we'd make a big island," Genifer says. "I think it came from traveling so much—staying in so many hotels, eating meals at the bar. It just makes such a great gathering space." The island they created is welcoming for guests and practical for the hosts, featuring eight bar stools clad in an unused vintage upholstery laminated for easy cleanup. The composition of art on the walls cleverly hides the fact that the television was accidentally installed

ABOVE The credenza in Lucy's room was a father-daughter design project. A mix of thrift-store art hangs above it. **BELOW** You don't need to spend years amassing a collection. Genifer purchased the white owls as a lot at an estate sale; they're on display in the built-in cases in the master bedroom and elsewhere throughout the house. **OPPOSITE** A cluster of simple paper lanterns adds a surprisingly elegant dose of whimsy to Lucy's room.

off-center. Still, it's the flaws that make a home more beautiful. "This house is not perfect," Genifer says. "It definitely has a lot of quirks. We're very detail oriented, but not everything is perfectly square. That's just the nature of life in a log cabin."

ABOVE LEFT A mix of the pretty and the practical on the kitchen's open shelves. ABOVE RIGHT Touches of kitsch (a cartoony bird, a pop print) are a quick and easy way to add fun and life to a room. RIGHT Oden, in superhero garb. OPPOSITE The kitchen—here, as in so many households, is the center of the family's home life.

THE CAREER OPPORTUNISTS

nine-to-fivers used to have the luxury of maintaining a clear barrier between their work and home lives, but the modern world's "conveniences" (the Internet, mostly) have erased the division between the private and professional spheres. That's not always a bad thing, as these residences demonstrate. It's not a matter of simply having chic home offices. What these fearless souls have accomplished is more nuanced than that; they've created a world all their own, one that's informed in equal parts by their private selves and their professional leanings. The results are enough to make you not just yearn for a new house, but dream of a new career as well.

A serene still life inside Kim Ficaro and James Wilson's Brooklyn apartment

TRUE SOUTH

VALORIE HART AND ALBERTO PAZ, NEW ORLEANS, LOUISIANA

Graceful, florid, a little dramatic—this New Orleans abode is a fitting home for a couple devoted to the art of the tango.

●

In 2005, Hurricane Katrina forever changed the landscape (both psychic and physical) of the city of New Orleans. Valorie Hart, recalling the immediate aftermath of that storm, says she dealt with her depression by hiding in the house and redecorating. "I could make it beautiful inside, even though it was so heart-breakingly ugly outside my door." A few years on, Hart's home in the Irish Channel neighborhood is testament to creativity and resilience—both hers and that of the city she loves. The home where she and partner Alberto Paz live and work is imbued with a heavy dose of New Orleans spirit, and she approached decorating with passion and romance, the very qualities that the Argentine tango, her chosen art (or one of them), is known for.

If you want to use the metaphor of dance, though, when it came to decorating, in addition to the extravagant gestures of the tango, Valorie was unafraid to improvise. The space they started with is a classic New Orleans double shotgun house. The shotgun is a native architectural form, usually a humble wood structure: a simple volume carved into a few rooms, with no hallway or passages between them. A double shotgun is, as it sounds, two such houses that share a common wall. It can be a challenge to adapt such spaces—originally conceived to be shared by multiple, often impoverished, families—to suit contemporary tastes. To make things a bit more challenging, this used to be a group home for girls, and had undergone a renovation by what Valorie generously terms "volunteers of varying degrees of experience." Naturally, the couple wanted a home that felt as far from institutional as possible, and to keep costs down, they chose to transform the house via its décor. "I'm a New Yorker," Valorie says. "Renting apartments for so many years taught me to use what I've got and make it beautiful."

What she got was a floor plan that's not to modern tastes, one in which bedrooms flow

In the dining-room-turned-office, cascading turquoise silk curtains are an electric jolt against the rich red walls. Lavish décor inside a humble home just makes so much sense in New Orleans, where grandeur and grit live comfortably side by side.

into one another (and in turn open into the kitchen), and myriad legacies of that amateur renovation, including mismatched doors and laminated flooring. But the decorating challenge was one to which Valorie was uniquely suited. As a dance teacher, she is accustomed to helping average people find their inner grace. Using patience and inventiveness, she was able to coax out these humble rooms' inner majesty.

The guest bedroom, for example, welcomes overnighters with an extravagant embrace, offering the fantasy version of an evening in New Orleans. The chamber is dominated by the big bed—"I think most people enjoy sleeping in a four-poster bed when they're on vacation," Valorie says. Rather than dress the canopy, though, she hung canvas drop cloths on the wall. As they now occupy all of a house designed for two families, Valorie and Alberto didn't require all the original doors and passageways. The drop cloths add a sense of softness and movement, as a dancer's skirt might, as well as accomplishing the more practical necessity of hiding an inconveniently located door to the adjacent master bedroom. Valorie employed a similar trick in the master suite, padding the shared wall, completely hiding the door, and upholstering over it with inexpensive burlap. It adds some rough-hewn texture, a nice counterpoint to the feminine flowing bed linens and the pretty slipcovered bench (where pup Cholo likes to curl up). The eye-catching headboard is in fact

ABOVE Valorie and best pal Cholo in the master bedroom. Here, too, lush fabrics on the windows and the bed add a sense of softness and romance to the space. BELOW The 1970s lamps were once pale pink. "One day I was thinking about alabaster lamps," Valorie says. "And somehow I decided to paint and faux marble them myself. I dragged them to the yard—it took me about an hour." OPPOSITE Even the humblest fabric—in this case, canvas, draped on the wall to obscure an inconvenient door—can add luxurious texture to a room.

the two ends of a Directoire daybed. Lacking room for the piece, Valorie disassembled it and mounted both ends to the wall as a headboard. Above hangs a seascape by Carlo of Hollywood, purchased on eBay. "The lone figure overlooking the vast water just summed it up, post-Katrina," Valorie says. "Plus, a painting from the sixties over a headboard from the 1700s just tickled my fancy."

Though each room has its own distinct personality, connective threads run throughout. While the linens on the bed and the floor-to-ceiling curtains on the window in the master bedroom recall the canvas on the guest room wall, what makes the home cohesive is more than subtle decorative choices. It's the humor. The juxtaposition of the camp painting and the antique furniture is a nod to the sheer unlikelihood of such elegant rooms in a shotgun shack. This larger context ensures that the house's rooms always retain a sense of lightness and fun.

The carefully laid out formal living room is the work of someone who takes décor seriously—but, again, not overly so. "I had that old thrift store sofa reupholstered in white faux leather I found on eBay," Valorie says. Across the room is a nine-foot-long credenza, a signed vintage Baker. What seemed like the patina of the piece's long life was, in fact, nicotine stains. Valorie liked the color, though, so after giving the piece a thorough cleaning, she

ABOVE The homemade altar perfectly illustrates her many interests and inspirations. BELOW Valorie cites a laundry list of influences with which she credits the city of New Orleans: "The old, crumbling and well-preserved architecture, the vivid colors from Europe and the Caribbean, the Catholic and voodoo culture, the Southern gentility, the free-wheeling bohemian and artistic culture, the Creole culture, the immigrant culture, the African American culture, the subtropical climate, the bon vivant attitude, the beautiful shops, the light, the vegetation and gardens, the simple day-to-day friendliness of the people here." OPPOSITE The living room features a mix of modern design icons and yard-sale finds.

painted it to recapture that hue. "A few people have been horrified at the ease with which I paint over old furniture," she admits—but then this is the same woman who disassembled a Directoire daybed to make a headboard. Such cheeky (and cheap) gambits keep the space from feeling lifeless, which often happens when one over-decorates.

In the sunny kitchen, the iron table is paired with some stately chairs from Spain, and clad in a Uzbek suzani. The effect is so elegant it's hard to believe the table's . . . heritage. "I pulled it from the street on trash day," Valorie says proudly. The skeleton hangings are vintage medical charts unearthed in a flea market in Lisbon, a simple souvenir on the one hand and a window into the residents' decorating process on the other. The house is all about mixing European classicism with personal treasures, about showing off the imperfections earned with age and indulging one's desire for whimsy. Look closely: one of the skeletons is sporting a Mardi Gras mask—a little symbol of New Orleans and a reminder never to take things too seriously.

ABOVE LEFT Valorie tempered papered over the laminate cabinets, removing the upper doors to display some of her collection of white ironstone china. "I thought it was whimsical," she says. "It's in keeping with our philosophy of using what we have." **ABOVE RIGHT** Valorie and Alberto on the porch. **OPPOSITE** Once upon a time the home would have had several fireplaces; now only this one survives. The carved lintel has also somehow endured in the house over the years.

LIGHT TOUCH

KIM FICARO AND JAMES WILSON, BROOKLYN, NEW YORK

Two outside-the-box thinkers wholly transform a humdrum New York rental—a personal (and professional) triumph.

despite its name, the Brooklyn enclave of Greenpoint isn't much greener than any other part of the city. The urban landscape largely disappears, however, once you set foot inside Kim Ficaro and James Wilson's sunny railroad apartment, where the pair have created serene, nature-inspired rooms that offer a respite from the city just outside. Like most of their fellow New Yorkers, the two are renters, but via careful decorating choices they've put their own personal stamp on the apartment. It's very much their home—though it could easily double as their résumé, as it so perfectly captures both Kim's and James's unique professional perspectives.

As a prop stylist, Kim is expert at getting rooms picture-perfect for magazines and other clients. James is the modern-day renaissance man behind the popular style blog Secret Forts who also works hands-on as a set builder. The on-the-job training that their careers have afforded them is evident all over the apartment, from the custom furniture James is responsible for to the various vignettes and small decorative flourishes Kim created throughout the rooms. These careful decisions helped the couple turn another run-of-the-mill Brooklyn apartment into a home that's more inviting than that which most renters are able to create.

"We're only able to do some cosmetic stuff to the place," Kim says. "But we did spend about three months working on the apartment." Fortunately, short of actual structural renovation, the easiest way to change a space was still an option: they repainted every one of the apartment's four rooms using luxe colors from England's Farrow & Ball. The rooms and layout are simple, without much in the way of architecture or interior structure, and the hue highlights the apartment's advantages: high ceilings and natural light.

One of the apartment's disadvantages was standard-issue linoleum flooring, found in the kitchen. Unable to replace it, the two decided

The front room is painted in Farrow & Ball's Blackened. "It's the perfect pale gray," Kim says, "inspired by smoke from a fireplace tinting the walls." The quiet tone is as unobtrusive as standard-issue white, but it adds a subtle, textured backdrop for the couple's myriad collections.

simply to obscure it. "This IKEA flooring looks like whitewashed planks," Kim says. "James layered it over the linoleum, and it changed everything." It's a quick fix, but a brilliant one, lending the room a much more polished and serious feel. The faux planks and the simple wooden furniture are suitable for a farmhouse, yet surprisingly apropos in Brooklyn. But of course this isn't a farmhouse; it's an apartment, and not a huge one at that, so the room must pull double duty. "We do use this room for dining and dinner parties," Kim says, "but a lot of the time we work at the table." The table itself is their work, a metal-and-plank piece that James built. The adjacent shelves display some of the tools of Kim's trade—but when you're a prop stylist, your office clutter is pretty chic. Though the room's not overstuffed, the residents of this apartment aren't exactly minimalists, either. The collections on display in this dining area include glass vessels and pure white ceramics—and both seem to disappear. In this context, the black botanical print feels very present but doesn't overwhelm.

Kim and James have the good fortune to occupy the rare New York apartment with

ABOVE LEFT The vintage bookcase hails from India. "I have a lot of objects and collections of things due to my job," says Kim. "The bookshelf gave me an opportunity to display the pieces I love." ABOVE RIGHT Kim and James in their combo dining/work room. OPPOSITE It's important to decorate from top to bottom; the Moroccan lantern overhead helps bring balance to the high-ceilinged room.

natural light at both the back and the front. The living room's windows are on the building's façade, and afford direct sun for much of the day. Stylistically, the room is in keeping with the kitchen—almost a variation on a theme. The walls are that same subtle hue, the floor again covered, though in this case by a sisal rug, and there are more tables by James. The pair in the living room has an understated, slightly industrial vibe that's balanced by the room's softer elements. Kim transformed what she terms the couple's "ugly modern couch" by simply covering it up. "I like mixing the two different kinds of fabrics," she says. "It's like something out of a French château." The mismatched fabrics have a casual appeal, while the pillows and the big floor pouf encourage guests to linger.

The living room features more of the couple's collections, but the star attraction is the art. The handful of pieces (grounded by the large white painting, a James Wilson original) are hung over the couch in an unstudied grouping that makes the art feel accessible. A few framed pieces hang above the desk in the corner in the same offhand way. The case between the windows is crowded with piles of magazines. Not unsightly, but not exactly orderly, they're a reminder that this is a real home, where people actually live. In the vignette on top of the bookcase and elsewhere in the room, Kim has again incorporated natural materials—a personal favorite and a subtle way to bring the outdoors in.

The drawback of the railroad apartment is, of course, that the interior rooms are often gloomy, and can be quite small. But despite the lack of windows, ample light spills into the apartment's interior spaces: their bedroom and another spot Kim refers to as James's room. "It's good for a man to have his own room," she says. Industrial shelves hold the family library, though there's also room for James's bike and surfboard. The walls are a slightly

ABOVE Kim has a knack for stylish still lifes; even her desktop clutter seems chic. OPPOSITE In the living room, soft textures— the diaphanous window shades, the nubby-linen desk chair, the buttery leather pouf—help make the space feel all the more inviting. FOLLOWING PAGE Multipurpose furniture is the key to stylish apartment living. The tables, which James made, can be pushed together, used alone, or can even double as extra seating.

darker shade of gray than in the two outer rooms, so the palette feels consistent but not boring, and grass cloth wallcovering masks the cheap hardware-store closet doors. The bedroom sits between this and the living room, almost unfettered by walls, which ensures an overall casual air. "I like white sheets and a neutral bed," Kim says—and her preference keeps the little space feeling subdued and restful. The only real ornament is a print by Hugo Guinness (a Christmas gift from James) and a fluffy sheepskin.

The home Kim and James have created seems so much greater than its physical limits of four modest rooms. It's thoughtful but not overthought. You can see both the inhabitants' considerable professional knowledge and the evidence of their real lives—the beauty lies in the balance between the two.

ABOVE RIGHT Wall sconces are a great solution in a tight space—these plug in, and don't require any wiring, so they're ideal for renters. **OPPOSITE** The industrial shelving might seem more suited to an office building, but when it's filled, the structure fades nicely into the background. "Before, we didn't have proper bookshelves so there were books everywhere," says Kim. "This is one of the best things we've done."

CAMERA READY

GRACE KELSEY AND KENYAN LEWIS, WARWICK, NEW YORK

A young couple who know a little something about putting their best
face forward work their magic on a graceful old homestead.

In years past, Grace Kelsey and Kenyan Lewis would have discovered the charming farmhouse they call home while on a Sunday morning drive, or via word of mouth, or thanks to an intrepid real estate agent. In this modern era, however, they went online. "We were looking to consolidate our living and work spaces and stop working around roommates," Kenyan explains. "We looked in Brooklyn, we looked in Queens, we looked in the Bronx. In the end, we found the solution on Craigslist": an enchanting 230-year-old home—sprawling by the standards of a pair of urbanites—set on fifty acres (including outbuildings) fifty miles from New York City. It's not a grand country manor, but instead a low-key former farm: a wonderful respite from city life, and a relatively blank canvas on which the couple have created a work of art. It's home as wonderland, reflecting both the occupants' professional leanings and their sense of fun, whimsy, and eccentricity.

Their day jobs inform almost every aspect of the house. Grace is well known as a model, and works on the other side of the camera, too, as a photographer and illustrator. Kenyan began his career as a visual merchandiser in retail stores and now works as a freelance stylist, running his own prop rental business. Their shared concern with appearances and visual harmony is on display almost everywhere you look. Though each decorating choice the pair has made feels calculated, it's not about work: it's about expressing their passions and celebrating the house they both love. Of course, it's a house that's easy to fall in love with. It's about as far from city living as you can get, from the charming Dutch door to the grandly proportioned rooms; from the many windows to the view of rolling hills beyond those panes. The house has a timeless, quintessentially American feel that is somehow a very fitting context for Kenyan and Grace's personal aesthetics. Call it kismet, but everything about the house seems to suit everything these two are.

On their fifty acres, Grace and Kenyan have created a fantasyland all their own. His collection of props, her collection of vintage clothes, and their shared love of the old and unusual contribute to the farm's playful atmosphere.

The house is big, but the couple hasn't had any difficulty filling it. Kenyan's work requires him to have an astounding variety of things, and they're everywhere: walking sticks and tattered American flags, beaten suitcases and wooden chests, all manner of vases and vessels, and other curiosities. Add in the couple's personal possessions (dapper Kenyan's collection of shoes and hats, plus DJ equipment and a hefty record collection; Grace's collection of vintage clothing) and the house is teeming. The one common theme that unites all of their collections is the heavy emphasis on the vintage and antique. What better context to display their collections than in a grand old home such as this? So the effect of all the stuff isn't overwhelming; rather, the place feels very lived-in, as though they've been settled there for decades, generations.

Fresh paint brings new life into the rooms (pale mint, a burst of warm terra-cotta)—the biggest change the two, as renters, could

ABOVE Kenyan does DJ duty. "We collect a lot of costumes, just for fun," Grace says. "We're both obsessed with the style and quality of vintage fashion." Taking a cue from art collectors who occasionally rotate their collection, she'll change which dress hangs on the wall from time to time. OPPOSITE Kenyan's props are displayed so inventively they never feel like clutter or chaos, though technically the bric-a-brac and furniture he keeps on hand for his clients are the equivalent of those unruly piles of paper on most people's desks. But his discerning eye and knack for creating interesting vignettes ensures that even though much of what's in evidence is simply in storage until the next job, it all feels deliberate and offhandedly chic.

THIS PAGE The ducks were a gift from Grace's mom. **OPPOSITE** "This is supposed to be the dining room," says Kenyan. "But the tabletops are usually used for props either on their way in or out for rental." The vintage flag is a touch of Americana, a theme carried throughout the house. The display case is festooned with the logo of Kenyan's prop house; the pair sometimes sells small accessories at a friend's store.

commit to. A jolt of color awakens and unexpectedly modernizes the old-fashioned rooms, and stands in sharp contrast to the household's lovingly worn furniture, the majority of which is secondhand. The main living room's three cozy sofas were all eBay purchases, the dated upholstery proof of the adage that one man's trash is another's treasure. The key in this room is that the décor doesn't attempt to disguise or recontextualize the shabby couches. By pairing the couches with some elaborately printed curtains, a worn rug, and a liberal sprinkling of timeworn accessories (a vintage portrait, an antique camera, the house's gorgeous old plank floors) Grace and Kenyan make what should look like grandmotherly cast-offs seem downright chic.

Few young couples have need for three couches, but these two are consummate hosts, so ample seating space was a must, while the four bedrooms are a nice added bonus. "Working from home and being a bit of a hermit, Grace relies on people coming by to see her," Kenyan explains. "People visit quite often. We don't even have to invite them." The two kept the décor in the downstairs guest room understated, adding color and little else. Textured wallpaper is a good fix for renters; it disguises surface damages and can be painted again and again to suit a tenant's taste. The pale mint shade they settled on is serene, but present enough to make this otherwise spare room feel quite finished, with a vibe not unlike what you'd expect at a bed-and-breakfast. Their own bedroom is more effusively decorated, with pieces that hold some special significance, from the framed Maxwell Parrish

The couple's interest in the old and timeworn is evident everywhere, from the sculptural phonograph in the center of the living room to the treasure-filled shelves in the study.

print (which once hung in Grace's childhood home) to Kenyan's gorgeously sculptural antique hat stands.

Guests may come for a weekend respite from city life, but this is meant to be a home that strikes a balance between work and play. Both Grace and Kenyan log many hours in the comfortably laid-back office they share. The faux-weathered shelving is not original to the home, but something the current tenants inherited. The worn finish may be inauthentic, but it suits the home's down-at-the-heels chic, a vibe further enhanced by the comfortably dilapidated leather couches. Kenyan discovered those curbside on trash day, and paid the movers who were supposed to be disposing of them to deliver them to the house instead. "What most people call 'old' or 'used' we call 'enhanced' or 'lived in,'" Kenyan says. "We love our items to have a story to tell of their journeys through another lifetime, before they reached us."

ABOVE LEFT In the bedroom, a couple of Grace's vintage hats are displayed on Kenyan's antique hat stands. ABOVE RIGHT The red leather chair was found on the streets of Manhattan. Sometimes the clichés are true—one man's trash is another man's treasure. OPPOSITE A utilitarian fixture suspended from the exposed beams makes as big an impact as an ornate chandelier.

THE INCURABLE COLLECTORS

Crack open most decorating texts and you'll find a surprising amount of advice with regard to creating collections. The pros urge balance and harmony—and while there's a certain appeal in finding those three perfect Chinese vases (or whatever it is that strikes your fancy), it can be much more fun, and surprisingly chic, to indulge that inner urge to amass. These homes belong to voracious collectors who are unafraid to live with what some might term excess—and they do so beautifully.

Heidi Hough and Art Detrich's Chicago home

MORE IS MORE

HARRY HEISSMANN AND MARK KING, BROOKLYN, NEW YORK

Inside an average-size New York City apartment, one man has created a grand home stuffed to the gills with his myriad collections.

harry Heissmann's third-floor walk-up apartment in Brooklyn Heights is what most real estate agents might artfully term "intimate." But for Heissmann, who estimates that he and partner Mark King looked at about thirty places before buying, the one-bedroom flat possessed all the necessary qualities—prewar charm, ample light, and access to a roof deck. And, unbelievably, enough space for Harry to showcase his collections. For, leaving aside whatever other decorative gestures Harry has made in the small space—and there are plenty; a professional interior designer, he's got an impressive number of tricks up his sleeve—this is a home that is defined by its owner's collections. But since those various objets are so near and dear to his heart, the result is not just an apartment crammed full of bric-a-brac. It's unique, maybe a little unusual, but there's no denying that it's a home.

This isn't one of those sprawling, elegant apartments you see only in Woody Allen films. There's no foyer to speak of; you simply cross the threshold and enter the wonderfully weird world of Harry and Mark. An open shelf unit creates some division of the space, an improvised foyer of sorts, the resin Tony Duquette snail seated atop it a fitting first sight. The snail strikes the perfect note in a home where provenance meets pop, where luxury meets a bit of lunacy. The wall is tiled with mirrored squares, which emphasize the natural light from the nearby window. But one's first sensation isn't of light or air—it's of the overwhelming amount of stuff.

An extensive collection of all manner of pixies resides in the glass-front case, displayed as seriously as Fabergé eggs. And everywhere you look, there's something to see—books, art, curiosities, you name it. Beyond the improvised

"I started collecting when I was little," says Harry. "Things like shells and stones." But he was truly bitten by the bug when he accompanied his mother to a friend's house. "It was a castle," Harry recalls, "and full of antiques. I was in heaven, running around, looking at everything." Before Harry left, his host allowed him to choose one thing from the home to take with him. "I took a lampshade," he laughs. "Don't ask me why!" It wasn't just any old lampshade, but an Art Nouveau antique that may well have sparked Harry's lifelong interest in quality collectibles. Though when asked what inspired any of his current collecting passions, Heissmann offers the same reply: "Don't ask me!"

entryway is what Harry rather grandly terms the "dining gallery." This is the space where Harry (whose German upbringing is evident in a courtly manner that makes him the consummate host) prefers to entertain. "I think a banquette is so much more intimate than chairs," he says, so he had one custom-made; it is upholstered in a glitter silver vinyl that picks up the subtle effect he employed on the walls. To achieve the shimmer, glass beads were painstaking applied directly to the wall's surface. "The wall changes color all the time," Harry notes, "reflecting the light differently depending on the time of day."

In the apartment's main rooms, Harry aimed to balance glamour with the home's realistic scale, and to create a space that's a showcase for his eclectic taste. In the cozy living room, which is separated from the dining gallery by a pair of glass doors, classical symmetry and pieces with an impressive provenance (glazed earthenware brackets from the estate of the great French decorator Madeleine Castaing, a snail-shaped terra-cotta garden stool, a pair of 1940s altar candlesticks) find a sharp contrast in the kitschy fake fireplace and pop pieces by Takashi Murakami, Bob Mackie, and Keith Haring. "When I shop for my clients," Harry says, "I get to fulfill my fantasies, buying things I could never afford." Shopping for his own home is a more delicate balancing act, in which he pits his budget against his taste, thus more often than not opting for something witty and fun, not serious.

On display in the kitchen is the particular pride and joy of Harry's collection: a dazzling array of Sprout

The mirrored wall tiles create an illusion of more space, while the banquette saves room in the narrow dining gallery. The table was purchased at auction from Enron, the failed energy corporation.

memorabilia. Visitors can be forgiven for wondering, first, who Sprout is, and second, why Sprout instead of seashells, or stuffed bunnies, or Delft porcelain, or Brice Marden paintings, or any of the many things one could collect.

The *who* is easy to answer: Sprout is the animated sidekick to the legendary advertising icon the Jolly Green Giant. The *why* is more elusive. "I saw a Sprout lamp in a vintage toy store," Harry says. For whatever reason, it made an impresssion. "I began looking for things with Sprout on them, and started seeing them everywhere. Once you discover something you want to collect, you find it everywhere. I scooped up every single one." Harry resists any further analysis of why, and it doesn't matter anyway. For whatever reason, this little fellow awoke the collector in him. At this point, he believes he's amassed an almost complete collection of all the world's Sprout-related ephemera.

Since he can't splurge on museum-quality treasures, Harry instead indulges his design

ABOVE, LEFT AND RIGHT The previous owners renovated the kitchen with IKEA cabinetry (the ubiquitous stainless steel and frosted glass are the twenty-first-century version of the avocado-colored appliances of the 1970s) but Harry breathed life into the space with roman shades made of vintage fabric and his collection of 1950s-era Holt-Howard pixie jars. "I don't set out to buy things that are good," Harry says. "That's not my world." By which he means a complete set of vintage mid-century pottery is significantly easier to come by than eighteenth-century Meissen teapots, but no less rewarding to own and display proudly. **OPPOSITE** A selection from Harry's prized Sprout collection.

LIGHTHOUSE FOOTWEAR
Reptile Shoes

instincts, toying with his many objects and getting creative with his limited space. In this room, as elsewhere, he also rather boldly had wallpaper applied . . . to the ceiling. "There's nothing worse than having wallpaper die at the ceiling," he says. Lacking crown molding to define the space, he simply kept going. It's a move that challenges the received wisdom of decorating, but it more than pays off. "People always say, 'I would never do that!' but I think it gives the room more dimension. I'm a big fan of doing *something* with the ceiling."

This room, like the others, is full of things, but they're not there just because Harry has them—they're on display. Everything that's out is meant to be seen, studied, admired. The sheer amount of stuff is dazzling, and it's almost impossible to see it all in one go—which is part of Harry's gambit. He's lavished care and attention on every surface, and behind every corner. It doesn't matter that he's got only a few hundred square feet to work with; he has decorated his home as if it were a palace.

The exuberance that defines the rest of the apartment continues inside the couple's bedroom. The rich turquoise walls (a simple

ABOVE A floor-to-ceiling curtain (in the same print seen on the all-over wallpaper) obscures shelves that store odds and ends not on display. **OPPOSITE** Rules are made to be broken—a garden stool works just as well as a regular old coffee table.

THIS PAGE There's something to see wherever the eye happens to land. OPPOSITE The wallpaper creeps right up the walls and onto the ceiling. Rather than making the room feel cramped, it actually helps the space feel more finished.

ABOVE Harry displays less serious collectibles like Sonny & Cher memorabilia and the Sprout lamp. OPPOSITE A selection of tramp art frames is displayed over the bed. The American folk form was popular in the early twentieth century; decorative pieces were fashioned from cast-off cigar boxes and other scrap wood.

standard Benjamin Moore hue that Harry applied himself) are the perfect, soporific shade—and are offset by the hallucinatory iridescent holographic vinyl with which Harry lined the ceiling. (One imagines that looking up at this ceiling would feel very much like dreaming.) The 1970s light fixture—"It reminded me of a Slinky," Harry says—is a modern counterpoint to the array of wooden frames fashioned from cigar boxes, an example of native folk tramp art; they hold a selection of family photographs, works by Pierre et Gilles, and an illustration of Harry and Mark by their close friend, the illustrator Robert de Michiell.

Though a bit tongue-in-cheek, there's nothing ironic about the way Harry incorporates pop images: Cecil Beaton's portrait of Marilyn Monroe hangs in the bathroom (which is papered in the same print that appears behind Marilyn), Robert de Michiell illustrations of Cher show up in the living room, and Bruce McBroom's iconic shot of Farrah Fawcett is screened onto a bed pillow. In Harry's world, these women are the modern-day version of the Three Graces. There's a sense of classicism—particularly an emphasis on symmetry—throughout the rooms, lending order to what, in less capable hands, could easily become chaos. But the defining characteristic of this home is simply fun. "When Mr. Hadley came to visit," Harry says, speaking of the legendary American designer Albert Hadley, for whom he worked for almost a decade, "he said my home should be called 'the house of friends.' Because if you look at the things I collect, they all have eyes, a face, a personality. He was right. So I call these things my 'friends.'" Indeed, Hadley was right. It's a small apartment, but in Harry's capable hands, and thanks to his unique vision, it has become a home, full of light, energy, and, yes, friends.

THE URBANITES

HEIDI HOUGH AND ART DETRICH, CHICAGO, ILLINOIS

Inside a sprawling downtown Chicago space, one truly inventive couple has created a home around some most unusual prized possessions.

american cities have had a long and complicated life cycle. It can be difficult to imagine that only a few years ago many urban enclaves where yoga studios and organic bakeries are now de rigueur were significantly different places: abandoned, abused, and, quite sadly, forgotten. Urban renewal is a complex process, but the engine that always drives it is people. A city is only as strong as its inhabitants, and it's hard to think of a couple more representative of the spirit and attitude that can resurrect a long-neglected neighborhood than Heidi Hough and Art Detrich, who have made a truly iconoclastic home in Chicago's Wicker Park. It's a home that reflects its owners' passions perfectly. For Heidi, that passion is gardening; for Art, it's cars—and their home is in every way designed around those particular obsessions.

Their primary requirement when buying a home wasn't a good neighborhood or ample light or a particular style of architecture. "Art was paying rent at about six different garages," Heidi says. "We wanted to bring his cars under one roof." They needed enough space to house Art's auto collection, and they found it in a former social club in Wicker Park, which was a decidedly different neighborhood two decades ago. But they looked past the gangs and the trash, put down roots, and set about making a very unusual nest for themselves. Though they did rehabilitate the large space extensively, theirs is very far from the standard industrial loft conversion, because when Heidi speaks of bringing all Art's cars under one roof, she's speaking literally: Art's collection of vintage Jaguars occupies pride of place. The couple lives around them the way collectors might live around their Richard Serras or Mark Rothkos.

Of course, it's not unusual to design a home around a beloved painting or a piece of furniture. But a car? Or, more accurately, a fleet of cars? "In 1963, I lived outside of

"I don't consider myself a gear head," says Art. "Life's too interesting." His passion for cars is an appreciation not just about the engineering but also the aesthetics. In this unusual home, the car is just another thing of beauty, just another reminder of the past, not unlike the tin ceiling overhead.

Chicago. I ended up driving my next-door neighbor's Jaguar XKE to the prom," Art recalls. Some people marry their high school sweetheart; for Art, high school is where he discovered his passion for English automotive design. Asked to pinpoint what it is he loves about the cars, the normally voluble Art is succinct: "It's just beautiful design," he says. It's a reasonable enough argument. If you design your home around something you love, you'll end up with the home that suits you perfectly. There's no sense letting the fact that the thing you love is a car stop you.

To accommodate the cars and celebrate all that unfettered space, the couple opted not to put up many walls. A partition divides the kitchen from the main living area, but other than that, the graceful columns are all that define and give architectural structure to the expansive space. Instead of carving out rooms to create the creature comforts of home, the couple added a trailer to their mini fleet. "We just loved the Airstream at first sight," says Heidi. "It was like a piece of sculpture." It's more than decorative, though; it's their master bedroom. The sleek, jet-age lines have an undeniable appeal, and the trailer is in keeping with the theme already established by the cars on display. Another vintage Airstream stands sentry in the back garden, ready to receive guests. Perhaps it's because they're displayed so confidently, as though it's totally normal to have vehicles in the living room, that

In open loft spaces, it can be a challenge to decorate in a way that's appropriate to the scale—a challenge Heidi and Art have risen to by decorating around his collection of cars.

the trailer and the cars seem simply like design flourishes, and are no more out of place than a hearth or French doors might be.

There are no rules or conventional wisdom governing this sort of home as hybrid loft and garage living. Because the homeowners weren't working from a template, within an already understood form, they were liberated to just feel their way forward, decoratively, to allow for happy accident. This concept of home is an ever-evolving one. "We're inveterate auction-goers, street scavengers, and street sale attendees," Heidi says. "It is much harder to divest than it is to acquire, but when we accumulate too much stuff, we have a big old street sale." It's home not as product but as process.

Despite the open floor plan and the elements that aren't traditionally homey, Heidi and Art have surrounded themselves with pieces that wouldn't stick out in a proper town house—or, more accurately, several different town houses, as their decorative choices span an impressive gamut. There's Mission furniture inherited from Heidi's family, paired with iconic midcentury pieces. There are natural history oddities (the grand sailfish—"caught

ABOVE The Airstream doubles as the bedroom. OPPOSITE "Art likes to say that I caught the sailfish," says Heidi. "But I caught it at auction." The big fish is complemented by a variety of other natural specimens on display on the shelves below.

at auction," as Heidi says; the skull; the bone); there are modern art experiments (the neon sculptures above the kitchen, the cast of a female figure); there are beloved found objects, such as the stained-glass window discarded by a neighbor. Clearly the lesson is simply to collect what you love—disparate elements can complement one another in an unexpectedly chic way. Perhaps the décor works because Heidi and Art have chosen to live with things they're truly drawn to, while maintaining a healthy distance from those material possessions. The plan is, someday, to get rid of it all—from the sailfish to the Jaguars. This isn't a home about aesthetics; it's about personality, so even if they stripped away all the excess, Art and Heidi would still be perfectly at home . . . with each other.

Much as the two were not bound by walls or rules, their lifestyle is not bound by the reality of city living. On their tiny urban plot, Heidi has created the sort of garden you'd expect to stumble across in Northern California, not in downtown Chicago. "I started gardening about forty-five years ago," she says. "I still remember the first radishes I planted, and how stunned I was when they came out of the ground." Thus inspired, she immediately set about turning the backyard into her own slice of earth. "When we first came here, the backyard was a tire dump," she recalls. "I planted some ivy, which is every-where now, and some bird planted this giant mulberry

ABOVE "This building was sort of a Puerto Rican social club," explains Heidi. "Over the years we've met a lot of people who had graduation parties and christenings here." **BELOW** Even though it was full of good vibes, there was not much else about the space that was salvageable. "Every house we lived in my father either designed or redid himself," recalls Art, "with me working right beside him." **OPPOSITE** That early hands-on education has more than come in handy. "In twenty years, I think we've paid for only three things to be done in the house," Heidi adds.

tree which is now towering over us." In search of more sunlight, she eventually transferred her operation up onto the roof, using a system of sub-irrigated planters.

The courtyard garden is an essential part of the couple's life. "We keep those garage doors open nine months a year if we can," Heidi says. "We love to have friends come over, take things from the roof, and have a big old cooking session. We have extraordinary memories of being here with friends over the years. I just think that's the best thing in life."

ABOVE AND RIGHT Heidi's rooftop garden yields a bounty of produce. **OPPOSITE** Her backyard garden is strictly for pleasure.

into the living room, where the walls are neutral, the only color provided by the many beloved pieces Caitlin has acquired over the years.

Much of her collecting has focused on items that embody Caitlin's New England upbringing. These touches of the Northeast include the spool étagère by the front window, the model sailboat atop it, and the pillows fashioned from vintage boat flags, which show up throughout the rooms. Caitlin has addressed New England extensively in her art, too, dissecting the popular myths of America's early settlers and teasing out the dark side of our colonial forebears in eerie, unsettling dioramas and narrative hooked rugs. Her present work has evolved away from that preoccupation with her personal history as a descendant of a Mayflower Pilgrim, but Americana is still an important touchstone, and examples of it are found throughout the home. It's a funny juxtaposition—this quintessentially New England décor in a sunny Southern California home—but the stylistic contrast pays off beautifully.

For a period, Caitlin, an inveterate flea marketer and treasure hunter, hosted private sales of objets she'd accumulated. "I would go collecting things to sell," she recalls. "Then I just couldn't. Having trunk sales was great in theory, but sometimes I'd have such an attachment to certain things." The fruits of her fevered collecting show her interest in both the local (the vintage state

ABOVE The pillows are made from vintage boat flags. **BELOW** Stripes are a relatively easy paint treatment that yields a big graphic impact. **OPPOSITE** The patchwork of colorful glass panes signals the hodgepodge that awaits visitors inside. **FOLLOWING PAGE: LEFT** Nautical motifs appear throughout the house. The étagère is made from old spools. **RIGHT** Vintage signage is as suitable for hanging as fine art.

flag draped across the couch, the festive Mexican masks atop the cabinet) and the global (the ornate Indian wooden cabinet). These days, Caitlin finds inspiration in the natural world, and her work incorporates found objects that convey a sense of beauty without much intervention on the part of the artist. It's undoubtedly the influence of the rich natural beauty of Southern California, and traces of this newer passion are found everywhere. Caitlin uses shells, feathers, nests, and the like decoratively but simply, allowing these examples of nature to speak for themselves. Her vignettes imbue these items with totemic significance, while adding visual texture to the home.

Caitlin's private library is as filled with color and treasures as the home's living room. "I wanted to make my own little version of the library in the house I grew up in," she explains. She matched the gray color scheme to the one in her memory, and the exuberant embroidered Indian door panel and crisp white floor add an energetic jolt that balances out a color that could have been a dour choice. The little writing table is painted in the precise same yellow as the front door, tying the room thematically back to the house as a whole. Repeating motifs—a color, a shape, an object—guarantee that a home feels harmonious. The spare room, used for both overnight guests and meditation, feels connected to the rest of the

A coat of paint can change the walls—and the furniture. A bright yellow breathed new life into a table purchased at a flea market.

house through decorative touches on display in the living room, such as the boat flag pillow and the bird and fish illustrations. The floors here are painted as well—not white but a deep hunter green.

After the exuberance of many of the home's rooms, Caitlin sought a different tone in the bedroom. "I just wanted a clean, calming environment," she says. "The rest of the house is colorful, but I wanted something more neutral." The subdued space does feel markedly different, a retreat from the dazzling farrago in the rest of the house. The simple canvas-colored walls have a subtle depth of color, and Caitlin has been more discerning here, decoratively, incorporating only a handful of beloved pieces: a painted Indian armoire, a worn-in corduroy arm-chair, bedside tables purchased at auction. This home is stimulating and vibrant, and it needs this room's more restrained décor as a corrective. Her bedroom helps Caitlin appreciate the rest of the house, much as white walls in a gallery help viewers better see the art.

Perhaps the home's most startling space is, tellingly, the one to which Caitlin did the

ABOVE LEFT Caitlin in the kitchen. ABOVE RIGHT Even her cooking essentials are displayed quite deliberately. OPPOSITE The kitchen is a study in Caitlin's decorative interests: nature, as seen in the wall print; vintage, as with the floor lamp she found in her parents' basement; and family, as in the kitchen table, which was made by her grandfather.

least: the downstairs studio where she works. The gorgeous leaded window was one of the original details that enchanted her when she first saw the house, and it remains the room's dominant architectural feature. She added the staircase (it's no longer necessary to go outside in order to access the studio from above) and the storage underneath it. The studio is the perfect neutral setting in which to consider the variety of the resident artist's work, from the large-scale bear that towers over the room to the intimate collections of deliberately arranged natural and found objects. Caitlin conceives of her work as having followed a particular trajectory, from narrative and historical concerns to a current preoccupation with chance finds that embody the beauty of nature and her surroundings. That evolution strikingly parallels how Caitlin found the house itself. The previous owner sold it without an agent, and Caitlin simply happened to see it advertised on a flyer in a coffee shop. It was not unlike finding a seashell on a beach or a treasure at a flea market. It was all by chance, yet, as Caitlin puts it, "Buying this house was one of the greatest things I've ever done."

BELOW Caitlin purchased several blue-and-white porcelain jars in LA's Chinatown and had them wired into lamps—instant antiques. They show up throughout the house. OPPOSITE In the bedroom, color, not clutter dominates.

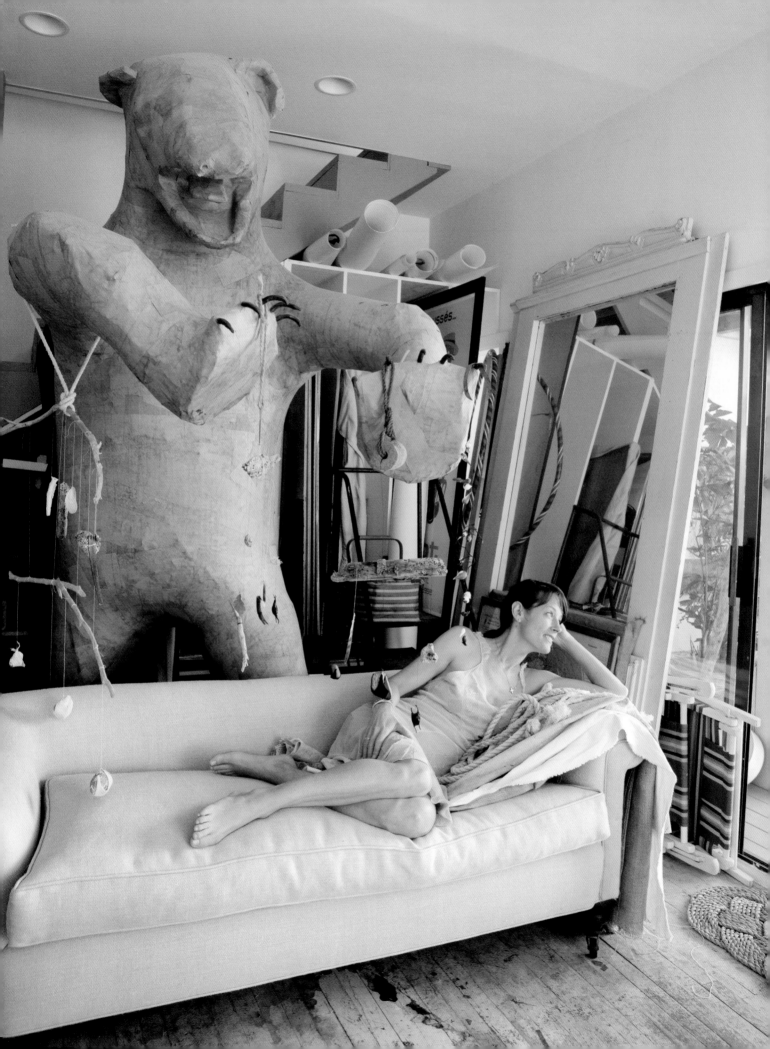

THIS PAGE Caitlin's workspace is a visual feast—collectibles, curiosities, tools, and oddities are scattered everywhere. OPPOSITE "The bear," says Caitlin, referring to the oversized creature that dominates the studio. "I just wanted to make a giant bear. I had no idea what I was doing, but I was obsessed with making this thing."

THE IMPERFECTIONISTS

modern life can be messy. Those of us who don't live in mansions with around-the-clock staff have to master the art of juggling housework and careers, responsibilities and relaxation. Add into the mix the chaotic reality of life with kids, and the dream of a picture-perfect home seems very remote indeed. But perfection is overrated. These homes don't have pristine spaces or flawless furniture, but their sense of vitality and surprise nevertheless makes them beautiful.

Beautiful disarray inside Erica Tanov's California home

LOFTY AMBITIONS

CHRISTIANE LEMIEUX AND JOSHUA YOUNG, NEW YORK, NEW YORK

Forget styles, forget periods—all I wanted from my Manhattan apartment was a place for my family to feel truly at home.

It took me a while to realize it, and it might seem like a surprising confession (given that I run a company aimed at making everyone's lives a little more chic), but style doesn't mean perfection. It's not what you see in magazines; it's more complicated, more attainable, and essentially whatever you decide it is. Case in point: my style is about trying to reconcile my appreciation for exceptional design with the fact that I've got a real person's budget—not to mention two kids, a big stubborn dog, and a company to run. But I've balanced these day-to-day pressures and considerations with my desire to live well, and in the end, I haven't had to sacrifice anything at all—because I've found the fabulous in what I used to think of as the flaws.

When we bought our place in New York it wasn't much more than an empty box. That's true for most of the loft spaces in Soho, where we live, and it's also kind of the point. Why live in a space like this if you don't intend to acknowledge the loft's industrial heritage? If it's pristine surfaces and plenty of rooms you want, you'd be better served moving to the suburbs. Though I had very briefly toyed with the idea of carving the space up into a warren of smaller rooms, an attempt to turn the apartment into an ersatz London flat, I'm glad I came to my senses. While it's fair to push yourself stylistically, it doesn't make sense to embrace wholesale an entirely different decorating language. (I could cram the apartment full of suits of armor and wood furniture, but it will never be a Bavarian castle.) It just made more sense to decorate a loft as a loft, so our décor emphasizes loft living's essential qualities: big windows, open spaces, high ceilings, and the exposed inner workings of the building. The trick for me was to balance those gorgeous old details with the demands of modern life, particularly modern life with a couple of kids.

When my husband, Josh, and I began our renovation, we were expecting our first child.

A clean white kitchen and metals stools with black cushions— certain combinations never go out of style. The Bertoia stools appeal to Mom and Dad's love of the classics, but they're also a cozy perch for the home's younger residents.

(What can I say? I love a challenge.) Undergoing the construction and then the decoration of the apartment at that time proved surprisingly helpful. I learned to see the world through the eyes of a mother, and that perspective influenced so many of the decorating choices made in the house. And five years later it continues to—as the kids grow (my daughter has a little brother now), I try to evolve with them, changing the décor to reflect our changing needs.

When you step inside the apartment—once you kick your way through the pile of abandoned shoes and jackets—you're greeted with, mostly, floor space. The floorboards were salvaged from an industrial building in the Netherlands; they have a rich patina, and are so beautiful that I didn't think it was necessary to bother with too many rugs. But most important, they're unbelievably durable. We live in Manhattan, so just running out the door and into a front yard isn't an option. Preserving some open space for play was one of my big priorities; my kids and their friends ride their tricycles all over the apartment with impunity. But we grown-ups live here, too. Open space can be a luxury, but it

ABOVE Kids are most interested in wide-open spaces. The leather chair is one of a pair found at the ever-popular Brimfield Antiques Show. **OPPOSITE** Scale is an important consideration in any space. The loft's décor has to balance both the high ceilings and the small stature of half of the home's inhabitants—hence the large painting, paired with the tiny pouf.

can also overwhelm. It's helpful to use furniture to define living areas, to create a sense of borders in the absence of walls. I've done just that, creating zones: a living room for entertaining and chitchat, a sitting room for curling up and watching TV, a dining room.

The area near the apartment's front windows is what we call the living room. The couches are simple and unobtrusive, but most of all comfortable. When you're decorating around a couple of little ones, you don't really have the luxury of statement furniture. The slipcovered

ABOVE The hearth's clean straight lines are balanced out by the gentle curves of the urn. OPPOSITE The subdued hues of the large painting pop boldly in the otherwise neutral space, which favors texture over color, from the plush rug to the velvet throw pillows.

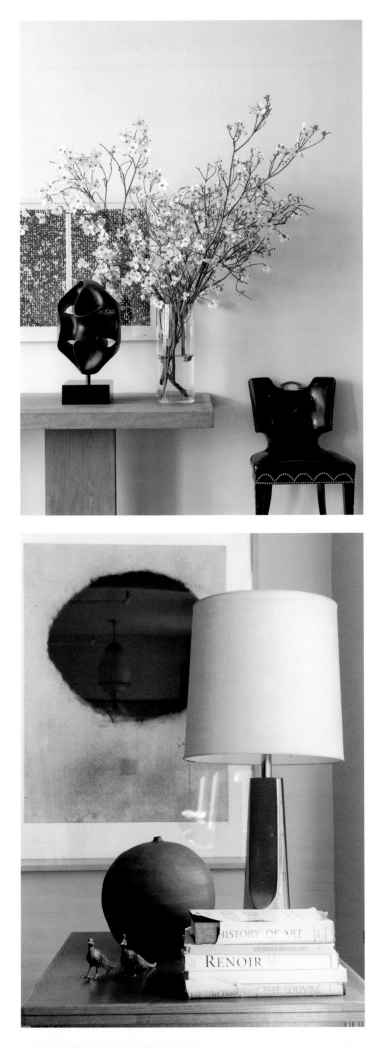

armchairs are a temporary member of the household, but there's something almost accidentally chic about the loose-fitting upholstery—it adds a bit of softness to a space that's otherwise full of hard surfaces and straight lines. The Robert Swain painting on the wall behind the chairs reinforces the precise geometry of the loft. The coffee table's round silhouette also helps counterbalance all the otherwise severe lines. And frankly, with two little kids and untold numbers of their pals running around the house, I'm terrified of edges and corners. I haven't intervened much, decoratively, with this space. The tall windows mean plenty of natural light, and there's a surprising amount of color and depth in the interplay between the crisp white walls and the complex finish of the floors. There's an irony here: given all this space with which to play, I've discovered my inner minimalist.

The sitting area is fairly simple: a sprawl-inviting sectional (with plenty of cushions for impromptu fort-building) faces the fireplace and TV, that modern-day hearth. The timber ottoman refers back to the wood beam overhead, which runs the length of the main room, the wood striking a warm note against the simple white couch. This area is pretty far from the front (and only) windows, so lighting was important. There's a lot of ambient spillover from the kitchen just beyond, so the simple tripod lamp is sufficient here—perfect for curling up with a book. Because this area is more casual, and

THIS PAGE Various still lifes are subtle but still eye-catching: the silhouette of the Judy Jackson vase mirrors the shape in the artwork behind. The art above the console and in the living room were both purchased at auction, from the estate of the choreographer Merce Cunningham. OPPOSITE The loft's skeletal system is entirely exposed—but painted black and white, to coordinate with the rest of the décor.

because at least half of the household enjoys simply lying on the floor, I added a rug. Some parents might recoil at the pairing of the white rug and couch and two small children. Not us. No grape juice is the only rule—these days, there are solvents and potions strong enough to banish any other stain.

The kitchen was something we created wholesale, with new cabinetry and the great big center island, which was key for prep space and a place for simple meals. (It's also nice to have a great big flat surface for art projects.) The dining table is in plain sight of the kitchen, so no matter what I do, dinner parties are going to be a casual affair. Thus I amped up the elegance, with a huge, antique dining table I discovered at the Clignancourt flea market in Paris. It's incredibly wide by modern standards—it dates from an era when no one had to pass anything to their fellow diners; there were servants on hand to attend to such matters. Though some might be fearful of using an antique in a household with two little kids, the truth is that in centuries past, craftsmen built things to last. My kids absolutely love to play at the table, whether it's building a fort underneath or planning a party on top. We have all this room to play, but somehow kids like small spaces . . . I guess we're den animals at heart. If that table could survive what the last century had to offer, I'm confident it'll hold up until my children are

Balancing the old and the new, the antique table is paired with modern dining chairs—and punctuated with the glorious cascading chandelier.

sheep covers up the hole in the wall where the cable used to connect to the guest room TV. I'm all about the decorative quick fix.

The only objective in the master bedroom was to create a retreat from the workaday world. The extravagantly textured rug makes the industrial space feel warm and inviting, while the bed and nightstands have the same simple, classical lines as the rest of the furniture in the apartment.

Here, too, the walls are largely unadorned; one trick of loft living is that when you don't have a lot of rooms, you don't have a lot of wall space. I preferred to keep what walls we do have uncluttered and relatively calm. The key word here is *relatively.* Our apartment does have a serenity to it, but mostly when we're not at home. When we are, it's full of noise, laughter, and song, the sounds of play and of life. That's just how I like it.

ABOVE LEFT We loved the original structural column in the bathroom. Loft living means embracing—and celebrating—architectural oddities. Josh wanted a big master bath, an homage to the one his parents had. The kids love to play in the deep tub, while Mom and Dad treasure the his-and-hers closets. ABOVE RIGHT Josh and Will. OPPOSITE In the bedroom, neutral tones—the simple white shades, the light-beige headboard and rug—are a subtle backdrop for the statement-making bedding and the chandelier overhead.

BACK HOME

CHRISTINA SACALIS AND KURT STEINERT, STOCKTON, NEW JERSEY

This inventive couple has managed to create a startlingly beautiful retreat from the world, guided by a desire to live in harmony with their surroundings and create a magical place for their children.

"Years ago I left my hometown and swore I'd never return," says Christina Sacalis. "I couldn't wait to leave. Now I live four miles away from my parents. They still make fun of me for that." Christina, husband Kurt Steinert, and kids Emmett and Ila Pearl had hoped to settle in Pennsylvania, but the lure of their cozy abode in Stockton (mere minutes from Christina's hometown) proved irresistible. Despite ourselves, we often turn out just like our parents; perhaps it's becoming parents ourselves that helps hasten that transition. Christina has worked past her long-declared reluctance to go home again, perhaps finding there what her own mom and dad found there: a good place to raise children. But just because Emmett and Ila Pearl take priority doesn't mean the elder members of the household don't enjoy a chic and stylish life. In fact, their home is an astonishing rebuttal to those who argue that living with kids means living without style. It may not be an impeccable, flawless manse, but in its imperfection, Christina and Kurt have found more than just charm—they've found magic.

That sense begins before you even step inside the house. "You have to cross a footbridge to get to the front door," Christina says. "It's completely enchanting." The 1870s home sits on seven acres of fields and woods, and includes a barn and a chicken coop—a bucolic dream. But when the couple bought the house it had lain empty for a few years, its only residents field mice, its interior still bearing the telltale signs of a dated 1970s renovation. "The first thing we did was get a Dumpster. We ripped out everything—bookshelves from the seventies, carpeting, falling plaster," says Christina. "But we tried to save as much of the original as possible." For her and Kurt, part of being committed parents means being devoted environmentalists. Thus, when renovating they aimed to repurpose as much as possible, just as they

Entering the house requires crossing a bridge—a very literal marker that you're leaving one world behind and entering another place entirely. It's fitting—inside, Christina and Kurt have made a world all their own, a sanctuary from the noisy modern world.

ABOVE An old industrial cart is pressed into service as a very chic toy box. OPPOSITE The powder room door was found in the barn. Christina didn't want a door that would swing into the playroom, so she mounted it on sliders.

did when decorating—flea markets and vintage shopping are, after all, just another way to recycle.

After crossing the aforementioned footbridge, one enters the house, tellingly, via the kids' playroom. "I think this was originally the formal dining room," Christina explains, "but we're not formal people." It was important to the parents that the kids had a place to call their own, and equally important that the room reflected the presence of the grown-ups, too. The pair of tea-party-ready tables are just the right scale for young revelers, but their modern lines and natural finish are inoffensive to adult sensibilities. This room is instructive for parents, new and old—it's filled with things to keep the little ones busy, but it doesn't feel cluttered; it's alive with color (thanks largely to the patchwork rug), but it's not garish. It's kid-friendly but still chic, without the fussy preciousness of mini–Verner Panton chairs or the horrors of the cheap, throwaway furniture found in so many nurseries. Rather, there's an antique industrial cart, its shelves lined with art supplies, and a standing wire basket, also an antique, filled to the brim with toys.

The colorful bric-a-brac includes many classic favorites but not much in the way of modern, cartoon tie-in toys. "We're trying to raise the kids media-free," Christina explains. That means no computer games, no TV, and only the occasional movie. She acknowledges that this sort of diet isn't for everyone, and will be harder to maintain as the kids grow, but for now the parents feel they've made a very wise choice. "It's liberating," Christina continues. "I feel like the kids are so creative with their lives. They get to make up their own worlds, rather than have their play dictated by the media." That's not unlike what the family has done in their home: create their own world designed not according to any rules beyond a desire to tread lightly on the planet while also living beautifully.

The spirit of low-key, comfortable chic that pervades in the playroom extends into the home's other spaces. The living room isn't formal in the least, and certainly isn't reserved for high tea with visiting relatives. It's a relaxed, cozy room for when the family wants to read or nap. Its soft textures and loving touches are emblematic of the home's welcoming vibe, so it's a perfect room for entertaining guests. Christina found the couch at an unremarkable department store in New Jersey she's been visiting since her childhood. It's a workaday silhouette, rumpled and easy, but it delivers what one most wants out of a couch: comfort. Christina paired it with slightly fancier armchairs. "We've had those for years," she says. "They were the first pieces of furniture Kurt and I bought together. Now they're totally threadbare." No matter; the chairs wear their signs of age with pride. To make things even more comfortable, Christina draped small sheepskin rugs over both the couch and the armchairs.

Decoratively, the house remains a work in progress. "You have to live with a place," Christina says. "These things don't happen overnight." Thus, the vintage army cot near

ABOVE LEFT The threadbare cushions are testament to just how well loved the armchairs are. The distressed table behind reinforces the room's sense of worn comfort. OPPOSITE Inexpensive IKEA sheepskin rugs help make the living room's furniture even more inviting. The retailer is one of Christina's favorite resources—she laughs when recounting that IKEA was, in fact, Emmett's first word.

the fireplace may someday be covered with a comfortable ticking mattress, though for now it's just an interesting object, a sculptural touch that's perfectly at home amid the other pieces, such as the antique industrial metal shelves or the old sign unearthed at a yard sale. Taken together, it makes for a jumble, but a pleasantly comforting one.

The three bedrooms are outfitted in much this same patchwork of styles, with vintage pieces and a generally relaxed air. The kids' bedrooms are cozy and have touches of whimsy, but they're not babyish or silly. It's almost as though the parents have too much respect for their kids to saddle them with cheap temporary furniture, the stuff you find in most kids' rooms. In Emmett's room, the yard sale school map and giant letter *E* have a quintessentially little-boy feel, while Ila Pearl's room is girly but not princess-y. The rooms are designed for kids, but are chic enough for the teens the kids will someday become—the perfectly girl-size armoire and graphic striped pouf and rug are pieces Ila Pearl won't necessarily outgrow by twelve.

Though the house is by no means cluttered or busy, in contrast to the rest of the rooms, the master bedroom is especially serene. "Our house is full of the chaos that comes with having kids," Christina says. "I wanted our room to be pared down—a place to sleep." She kept the palette in this room even more muted than elsewhere,

The kids' rooms have a timeless sensibility—no TVs, no bedsheets emblazoned with cartoon characters. It's almost possible to imagine the kids of some earlier generation living here, but they're still as filled with delight and surprise as any child's room should be.

creating a space with timeless charm using such modern ingredients as an IKEA bed. She balanced the new bed with a vintage bench, used as a nightstand, another of several pairings of objects new and old. In each case, the store-bought things don't seem showroom-new or overly identifiable, nor do the vintage pieces look like serious antiques. Rather, the overall effect is subtler: everything simply fits, fading just far enough into the background. It's neither a picture-perfect magazine spread nor a humdrum page torn from a catalog—it's a real home.

The heart of this home is very much the kitchen. "In this neighborhood, everyone's house is an extension of your own home," Christina explains. "So neighbors just walk right in. We're constantly entertaining, in our own casual way." The couple carefully planned the kitchen to be as conducive to ease and comfort as possible. They used the rolling cart that now holds the playroom toys as a storage unit during the renovation, and they became used to easy access to everything they needed—hence the current open shelving. The kitchen straddles the original home and its 1980s-era addition; the irregular floorboards

ABOVE Ila Pearl takes in the yard. The paper flowers were decorations from a baby shower Christina hosted—the kids loved them, so they became a permanent part of the décor. **OPPOSITE** It's not always easy being green. "We were so excited about the organic mattress," says Christina. "But it's uncomfortable! It's like a slab." The couple layered on a soft mattress topper and other inviting linens.

in the room show precisely where the one ends and the other begins. Even the imperfections the renovation didn't address (including the large picture window in the adjoining dining area) have grown on the family, and now feel like just another part of the house.

It's in the kitchen that the family prepares the many vegetables they cultivate in their big garden, the blueberries that grow just outside, and the eggs they collect daily from the chicken coop. The act of eating locally—right out of your own yard—is probably the most environmentally responsible thing that happens in this house, but it's not done just for practical reasons. "We wanted our kids to have a genuine bond with the natural world," Christina says. "We thought the best way to do that would be to have a stream, and a garden, and chickens. You can't expect kids to care about this world until they fall in love with it."

ABOVE Christina found the antique pendant lamps in the basement of an architectural salvage firm in Pennsylvania. The open shelves feature a pleasant jumble of dishes and decorative pieces. **BELOW** Christina and Ila Pearl pick up something fresh for breakfast. **OPPOSITE** The mismatched flooring indicates where the original house ends and the 1980s-era addition begins.

FLAWED BEAUTY

ERICA TANOV AND STEVEN EMERSON, BERKELEY, CALIFORNIA

This Bay Area house ably demonstrates that perfection is vastly overrated.

f or those who've never been there, the name Berkeley, California, conjures up images of fierce political sentiment or the laid-back hippie life. It's true that the University of California–Berkeley campus remains one of the capitals of the American left, and that organic cuisine and green living are a matter of course there, but that's hardly the whole story. Berkeley is one of the most gorgeous corners of the country, and offers a model of how to live well in almost every sense of the word. Fashion designer Erica Tanov's home is representative of the city's laid-back approach, an example of a unique philosophy that conceives of a beauty that's more about flaws than fantasy.

Erica, who grew up in the Bay Area, shares the house with her husband, Steven Emerson, a musician who's also a California native; and their kids Isabelle and Hugo and pooch, Lily. The family had been in the market for a house in Berkeley for some time when they discovered the 1930s residence where they now live. "The light was so amazing. That's really what drew me to it," Erica explains. "And the house has incredible views. It's just wonderful to look out and see the bay." The family soon encountered a problem that's not uncommon to homebuyers: much-needed structural work, in this case, a new foundation, soaked up funds that might have otherwise been directed elsewhere. The lack of a decorating budget wasn't prohibitive, though; the home's inhabitants are incredibly adept at finding beauty in rooms many might have renovated.

The light that so seduced Erica is evident throughout the house, a connective thread that runs through every room. Sometimes the greatest decorative flourish is one provided by Mother Nature. The warm light (and not much else) fills the ground-floor sitting room. "When we moved in, this was an office that had been redone in the seventies," Erica explains. "There were built-in shelves and cabinets everywhere. We

In the sitting room, the bare walls have a weathered patina that's surprisingly charming. The Chinoiserie credenza was found at a local salvage yard. Throughout the house, Erica and Steven have overlooked the scars and smudges that would distress most homeowners, embracing imperfection and redefining beauty.

ripped it all down, and I was thinking of putting up wallpaper, but I liked these marked-up walls. I didn't want to paper over them." Imperfectly textured walls covered with splotches of plaster (and traces of some long-ago carpenter's graphite notations) may not be for everyone, but it's hard to deny that the effect seems somehow just right—infinitely more interesting than a coat of paint. By revealing the hidden layers, Erica pays homage to the home's heritage, to the life it had before she and her brood took up residence there.

The battle-scarred walls, the vintage daybed found on eBay (the dog spends so much of her time there the family has taken to calling this Lily's room), the 1960s Chinoiserie credenza ("I loved the funny little legs," Erica says), the flea market lamp dressed up with a shade from Urban Outfitters, the tattered rug—all these elements add texture and a sense of worn-in warmth to the room. This space is an object lesson in Erica's unique attitude toward decorating: mix history and humor, imperfection and the everyday. This blend is employed throughout her home; the shabby becomes the positively chic.

Erica achieved that signature feel in the

ABOVE Throughout the home, Erica creates still lifes and vignettes mixing natural touches and favorite objects in a casual, unstudied way. **OPPOSITE** In the sitting room, pieces from the family's large art collection await a turn on the wall.

plenty of built-in storage, but Hugo chose the Zachariah O'Hora painting from his parents' extensive collection that hangs above it. He's got favorite toys on display, however Mom tucks him into some positively grown-up Indian-looking bedding at night. The room feels like a little boy's realm, but Erica's influence is still present, so the space is of a piece with the rest of the house. In Isabelle's room, Erica exerts less control—"I might offer a suggestion, but everything in the room is Isabelle's idea." Even so, the vintage bed painted pink and the various fanciful vignettes and trinkets suggest that, whether via genes or osmosis, Isabelle has her mother's eye.

Though she runs her business from a studio in Berkeley, Erica does have a home office—for her fabrics, a library, and other treasures to keep her inspired—in what was once a sun porch. The tools of her trade and a few family snapshots are the primary decorative elements in the work space, along with the sunlight. The room is flooded with light and has what Erica aptly terms a "tree house" feel. The linoleum underfoot is a

ABOVE, LEFT AND RIGHT In Isabelle's room, color predominates, from the candy-pink of the bed to the striped rug to the bright orange pouf. **OPPOSITE** Hugo, in his room. The kid-sized bed is dressed in grown-up sheets, and he chose the painting above, from Mom and Dad's collection.

legacy of the previous renovation, and something Erica aims to change. The stopgap solution is a big, worn Oriental rug (one of many in the house), and in the larger context of the room the eyesore of a floor is barely noticeable.

Though her attitude toward decorating is fairly casual, Erica knows design—it's her business as well as her passion—and is unafraid of big, dramatic statements. In the master bedroom, a lavish handpainted Chinoiserie wallpaper by the storied French firm de Gournay pro-

Inside Erica's sun-drenched studio, even the tools of her trade and normal office clutter seem downright chic. "It's hard for me to describe my clothing," says Erica. "But I guess the words I'd use—peaceful, relaxed, refined, casual—apply to my home too."

vides an elegant counterpoint to the casual textiles on the bed. "I originally bought the wallpaper for my San Francisco store," Erica says, "but it arrived late, and I'd already hung a painting in the store. So I held on to it for three years before I could decide where to put it." It's the kind of wallpaper you generally find only in the European-inspired mansions of the very wealthy, and a favorite of professional decorators, but Erica treats it without any undue reverence. The silver leaf is tarnishing as it weathers, adding a rich patina to the already fine silk, which nicely complements the mismatched nightstands, both of which Erica found at the Alameda Flea market, one of her regular haunts.

Though throughout the house Erica and Steven have compromised on little aesthetic details, the kitchen is the

Printed wallpaper obviates the need for standard decorative touches like a headboard or art on the walls.

one room the two are certain they'll renovate at some point. The aim here was simply to create something functional and cheerful enough to last until they could undertake a big overhaul. "I wanted to work with what we have rather than fight against it," Erica says. Thus she added pieces in the existing color palette and focused on making things functional enough for dinner parties and weeknight meals. This was key, as entertaining is a big part of their family life. The couple regularly hosts house con-

BELOW An injured chair patiently awaits some TLC in the dining room—a clear indicator of Erica and Steven's laid-back approach to their home. **OPPOSITE** Erica and Hugo in the kitchen. Here, as in so many homes, is the heart of family life.

certs in their roomy yard, while dinner parties take place around their commodi-
ous dining table, purchased years ago for only $100. Behind the table, Erica has
hung a handful of the paintings in her expansive collection. In the dining room,
the collage features work by Elodia Muzzi, a great-cousin, and by Isabelle, alongside various flea market finds. Erica's method for hanging art is also an apt metaphor for her way of decorating. "I like to hang
an assortment," she says. "And sometimes I
just start where there happens to already be a
nail hole in the wall. It gives you a somewhat
haphazard feel, but it's like fate—the picture
just belongs there somehow."

ABOVE The family at mealtime. Behind, the art is hung
casually, almost haphazardly. **OPPOSITE** The dining room,
like the rest of the house, is filled with vintage pieces. "I love
auction houses and flea markets," says Erica. "It's not like
shopping in a store at all. You can find pieces from so many
places and so many times—it makes you wonder about the
history of your things."

THE SELF-STARTERS

among the reasons people hire designers is the chance to get a crack at their Rolodexes. There are pros for every project (creating a Japanese garden, rewiring antique chandeliers), and only the connected few always know whom to call. But there's another kind of person altogether: the one who picks up a hammer (shovel, axe, measuring tape, what have you) instead of a telephone. Sometimes the easiest way to get things done exactly the way you want them is to do them yourself, and these homes prove that sometimes taking the hands-on approach can be quite beautiful.

Natascha Couvreur and Olivier Azancot's coolly understated country house

FIRST SIGHT

CHASE BOOTH AND GRAY DAVIS, COPAKE, NEW YORK

This New York City couple breathed new life into a long-abandoned house with bold colors, impeccable furniture, and a lot of hard work.

Chance encounters can change everything. Unforeseen events lead to marriages and career turning points all the time, and for Chase Booth, heading out for a jog during a long weekend in the country led, eventually, to the now-gracious second home he shares with partner Gray Davis. But before the place was a retreat from the couple's responsibilities, it was at the top of their to-do list. Abandoned when they found it, the house needed their keen eyes and soon-to-be-expert hands to transform it into the inviting retreat it is today. The result is a home that physically embodies its owners (both structurally and decoratively), and is thus a place where they can truly feel at home.

The house is located in Copake Lake, a scenic spot in the foothills of the Berkshire Mountains. The couple was visiting a friend in the area when Chase stumbled across the home that would one day be theirs. "This place was just left to die in the woods," Chase says. "The ceilings were caved in; there were dead animals inside." But somehow the pair was able to look past the overgrown brush and years of accumulated rubbish and see potential. Among the detritus inside the house was a bundle of cash, clearly inadvertently left behind. Chase used the money to buy the couple's very first tools, which he proceeded to put to great use.

Chase had only a boyhood education in home repair, but he and Gray had spent all their available funds to buy the house, so he had no choice but to learn how to do things himself. "We literally grabbed hammers and started tearing down the ceilings," Chase recalls. "Then we just had to figure out how to get them back up." Now he's an expert (working as a set producer, he builds for a living), but it all began with the lake house—the weekend getaway is in many ways Chase's alma mater.

This is an unstuffy house in the country, so you enter right into the kitchen. The front windows and glass door afford a light, airy feel.

Furniture can be painted, rehabbed, and customized to suit your needs; to turn the credenza into a proper bar, Chase simply had a mirror cut to the piece's exact dimensions, totally reinventing it. The wall above is hung with family photos and thrift-store art.

To avoid compromising that, Chase and Gray kept the kitchen small, despite the fact that they both love to cook. There are no overhead cabinets and only simple, clean surfaces so that the kitchen, which isn't a room, recedes quietly out of view. "We didn't want it to feel like the kitchen was in the living room," Gray says. "Though, of course, it is." The kitchen may be small, but no matter: whoever is playing sous-chef can chop vegetables at the long dining table, and guests can mill around near the bar just across from the kitchen island.

The vintage credenza where cocktails are served was found in the nearby antiques mecca of Hudson. Chase added the mirrored top, imbuing the piece with an urbane, almost Art Deco vibe. The dark wood floors, which Chase himself laid down—at one point the home served as the office for the golf course across the street, and the floor had been completely destroyed by years of spiked shoes—have a similarly big-city sensibility.

They're unexpected choices in a simple cabin on a lake, but they gave the owners what they sought: balance. The sleeker elements have humble partners: the leather butterfly chair, the heavy carved wood chair, the safari stool, the burled wood table, the hide rug. The room bounces back and forth between city and country, and it's the tension between the two that makes it a success.

Chase and Gray have struck that vibe almost accidentally. "Initially, everything we bought was dictated by price," Chase explains. "A few years ago, no one wanted their grandmother's sixties and seventies furniture." Though the clean lines of the massive vintage sectional once felt dated, they now seem downright contemporary. The two scored that piece, the pair of white pleather armchairs, and the glass coffee table at an estate sale—for less than $200. This assortment of furniture has a long shared history; perhaps that's why the pieces coordinate so perfectly. The acid green hue is a bold statement in any room, and especially so in this one, with its whitewashed walls and ceiling, and it has an unlikely complement in the

ABOVE Chase fashioned the rough-hewn table behind the sofa out of some vintage machine legs and some wood. **OPPOSITE: ABOVE LEFT** The simple dining table is Chase's handiwork. "We bought table stands on the Bowery," he says, referring to Manhattan's old-school restaurant supply district. "The table is so ugly if you take off the tablecloth." **ABOVE RIGHT** Gray (left) and Chase unwind. **BOTTOM** The dark tone underfoot only further amplifies the sense of air and light in the downstairs living spaces.

blue-and-white rug underfoot. The room feels cohesive but not overly studied, and comfort has taken priority over aesthetics—which is probably why there are so many seats available. With a room this cozy, friends are bound to come calling.

Sometimes those friends stay the night, but that's not a problem, given the three guest bedrooms that await upstairs. "This house was built to hold as many people as possible with as few furnishings as possible," Gray explains. "It's incredibly efficient." On the second floor, there's a bedroom situated on each corner, affording everyone a healthy dose of natural light, though each has its own unique charm and personality.

Extra spaces—a guest room, a powder room—provide the opportunity for decorative play. Accordingly, Chase and Gray painted one of their guest rooms a brilliant Kelly green. The striking color is a departure from the subdued tones in the rest of the house, but it's not an unwelcome intrusion. "People are always so worried about picking colors," Chase says. "Paint is easy—you can always paint over it." The deep hue is hardly in bad taste; in fact, some might find the color soothing and sleep-inducing. Chase balanced the statement color with natural hues and textures on the door and underfoot, and left the ceiling the same shade as in the rest of the home, so the room doesn't feel entirely disconnected from its larger context.

ABOVE Chase and Gray weren't opposed to outsourcing some of the labor—the headboards in the guest room were custom-made. BELOW The guest rooms are also design labs, where the couple can experiment with color—the walls here used to be turquoise. OPPOSITE "Someone had the good sense to put in these windows," says Chase. "We love them—they have such a great, almost Japanese, look."

Across the hall, the master bedroom is flooded with unfettered light. "We don't like curtains," says Chase. "We like to wake up with the sunlight. I'm grateful to whoever had the sense to put in all these windows." The stately cannonball bed belonged to Gray's grandfather; its grand lines are tempered by the broken-in green armchair, unearthed at a local junk shop. Light is virtually the only thing with which the couple has decorated their room, save a sturdy potted plant that has some distant cousins just beyond the windows. The hardy plantings outside occasionally poke their way in. "Sometimes the wisteria will grow overnight and wrap itself around the bedposts," Chase says, laughing. "It freaks a lot of people out, but I like it. When we first saw this place, it was overgrown, and basically we're returning it to that state—to how the house was when I first fell in love with it."

The home has come a long way since that first glance—literally. Moving the entire structure allowed the owners to create a whole new foundation and what eventually became their beautifully appointed basement, and it was one of the only jobs they outsourced.

ABOVE LEFT "Downstairs, we used the same elements you see upstairs," explains Chase, "only treated really differently." Thus, in the basement level, the walls are dark and the floor is light. ABOVE RIGHT Bedside essentials. OPPOSITE The couple found the chairs abandoned by the side of the road. The sculptural fixture overhead is by Grant Larkin, and the firewood holder was designed by Gray.

"I didn't realize that it's actually possible to move a house," Chase says. "It blew me away." The resulting basement was principally conceived as a wintertime retreat. Though not original to the house, it was executed as a variation on the themes established upstairs. There's the same knotty pine paneling as in the rest of the house, but it's laid horizontally. In a further inversion, the walls are dark while the floor is a brilliant white. These playful details ensure that even this new space feels related to the rest of the home. The long couch was custom-made to fit precisely in the niche between the two support beams, and offers guests the perfect place to sprawl before the fire on a cold winter's day. Should the couple feel like having a working weekend, there's a home office, too. Though, in truth, they've worked hard enough, and virtually everything you see inside this home is testament to that.

ABOVE LEFT The downstairs addition features a workspace for Gray—though the outdoor lakefront space is far more inviting. **OPPOSITE** Chase and pal Nessie at play on the water. Chase is adamant that a renovation like the one he undertook is possible, no matter your level of expertise. "I wasn't skilled at all. It took so long before I understood that there were proper tools for every job. But it was a fascinating process of discovery. Read a book, ask at your local hardware store—you can teach yourself."

THE MINIMALIST IN THE COUNTRY

NATASCHA COUVREUR AND OLIVIER AZANCOT, SEBASTOPOL, CALIFORNIA

This San Francisco family skipped the frills and frippery of most vacation homes, opting to use their own unique approach in their sun-filled weekend retreat.

*C*ountry *house* is one of those evocative phrases that sets the heart aflutter, awakening visions of long autumn weekends by the fire, or summer morning walks on dewy grass, naps on an overstuffed couch, and leisurely meals around a long, rustic table. The sunny home that serves as a weekend retreat for Natascha Couvreur, Olivier Azancot, and their three daughters delivers all the quintessential creature comforts, but looks unlike almost any country house one could imagine. It's a dramatic aesthetic departure from convention, a sleek and minimal space that's wholly modern but undeniably inviting. It's comfortable but stylish, and in almost every way a reflection of the owners' unique vision and hard work.

Though it's a mere hour's drive from the family's primary home in San Francisco, the weekend house feels a world away, thanks to the geographic quirks that make summer in San Francisco a chilly, foggy affair while inland it's all clear skies and warm sun. As it should be, the house is the opposite of the family's city abode. But this once-ramshackle spot needed much love before they could start spending weekends there. "It looked kind of like a dump," Natascha recalls. "The kids would just disappear into the weeds." Fortunately she had the requisite skills—a decisive sensibility, a roll-up-your-sleeves-and-get-to-work attitude—required to modernize the 1970s-era home, which she did via some surprising and counterintuitive decorative choices.

The boldest move Natascha made was to impose a startling color scheme in the house: a gray exterior and a crisp black-and-white interior. There are pops of color, but the cool,

The palette of Natascha and Olivier's weekend getaway is almost exclusively black and white. It's an unexpected choice, but white doesn't necessarily have to mean stark; it can be serene and hushed, too—precisely what you want in a vacation house.

restrained palette predominates, distinguishing this from the standard-issue Sonoma County getaway. "Minimal colors help keep my head clean," Natascha explains. "I can't function when there's a lot of stuff around." By mixing in soft textures and allowing in plenty of warm California sunlight, she introduces comfort into rooms that some might find severe.

When you step inside, the house simply opens up before you; the open plan, in conjunction with the consistent color scheme, unifies the space. In addition to the white walls, Natascha laid the same gray floor tile throughout the home's public spaces. It was an aesthetic choice and a practical one. "The tile is perfect for pool water," Natascha points out, logically enough for a mother of three girls who are bound to leave footprints all summer long. The house resembles nothing so much as an urban loft, with columns or a couple of steps serving as the only real division between adjacent spaces. It's the ideal arrangement for a household with three kids, who often weekend here with visitors in tow—the girls and their friends can careen around, from the pool to the dining table to the TV room.

The dining room features a showpiece table that is long enough to serve a small army of weekend guests—as an added bonus, the dark color makes it all but impervious to stains. Natascha has a firm sense of what she likes. "I usually have an idea of what I'm looking for," she says,

Hide rugs are a mainstay of midcentury interiors; their surprising versatility adds a bit of rich texture that suits almost any room.

"and I'll search and search without finding anything like it anywhere." Unable to find a table big enough to suit her tastes, she simply made one herself. A bench, also Natascha's handiwork, allows the family to maximize the number of guests. The skylights overhead provide more than ample light, but for evening dining, there are the vintage pendant lights, originally designed not to hang but to illuminate outdoor advertising from below, an industrial touch that blends into the room seamlessly.

A long workstation is set up against the nearby wall—kids today can't fathom a long weekend away from computers, after all—nicely echoing the long lines of the dining table and the horizontal stripes painted on the wall above. Natascha has an uncanny ability to find the inner beauty in mass-produced pieces: The desk is actually two IKEA tables pushed together; the lamps on top of them were found at Target. The big-box stores are an overlooked resource; there's not a lot that they can get wrong about a simple table or unfussy lamp. The chalkboard wall is a playful touch, but still consistent with the home's larger style statement.

ABOVE LEFT Even the dishes coordinate with the larger color scheme. ABOVE RIGHT Wood, stone, and light are the home's dominant motifs. OPPOSITE The simple graphic paint treatment on the wall parallels the simple lines of both the dining table and the desks, and also brings dimension and interest to the room.

The living room was carved out of what was once the house's garage (which is why it's sunken), but the décor keeps it stylistically related to the adjacent rooms. Here again it's not so much about a color scheme as the absence of color. The walls, the ceiling, the furniture—they're all a brilliant white. Even the window treatments transform the view outdoors into a simple white plane. Natascha used the same shades in every room in the house, off-the-rack shades from IKEA that allow in copious amounts of sunlight while affording the household some privacy. She chose iconic modern furniture, but as in the dining room, she was unable to find a coffee table that suited her needs, so again, she made her own. The table here is constructed of a piece of wood painted white and cut to balance perfectly on two globes. It's a playful one-of-a-kind piece that does more than hold its own against the iconic Mies van der Rohe chairs: it tilts the room ever so slightly off-kilter, combining humor with style.

Natascha's abilities extend beyond the chore of assembling IKEA furniture or the craft of whipping up a custom-made table; she's also responsible for the art in this room. The large piece on the wall was constructed from a wood frame punctured with nails and then woven with different-colored yarn. "I wanted something big and colorful," she says, "but not too overwhelming." The colors are subdued, but in the context of this all-white room, they feel positively vivid. Beyond adding color and

ABOVE Natascha and her girls. **BELOW** The girls' shared bedroom is treated as a mostly functional space, because there are so many more exciting places to be other than bed. **OPPOSITE** The master bedroom. In this otherwise subdued context, the vivid orange of the bedspread and the wall art (Natascha's handiwork, naturally) fairly explodes, filling the entire space.

visual texture, the handmade piece is a personal touch that brings a little bit of the artist into the room.

The home's public rooms share a decorative sensibility, and the bedrooms are a variation on this theme. In the master suite, the flourish of color on the bedspread and walls feels grand and extravagant against the neutral white spaces Natascha prefers.

The home is understated, but a few idiosyncratic additions invest the rooms with a lot of personality—as in the front sitting room, where the logs that will someday meet their fate in the fireplace line the mantel like tchotchkes; or outdoors, where Natascha improvised a text art piece with some Plexiglas and letter stickers. It's an important reminder that sometimes it pays to listen to conventional wisdom—sometimes less really is more.

ABOVE By the pool, Natascha's predilection for decorating with white creates the impression that you're at a luxurious Miami Beach hotel, even if the lounge chairs are just inflatable mattresses covered with simple fabrics. OPPOSITE By adding only the barest minimum (platform beds made out of doors, partitions made of curtains) Natascha turned an outbuilding from a garage into a guesthouse.

MOVIE MAGIC

MICHELLE AND DAVE KELSEY, ABITA SPRINGS, LOUISIANA

Old-school treasures, inspired combinations, and some very impressive craftsmanship bring this rambling Louisiana abode to life.

there's a rumor that the house Dave and Michelle Kelsey share with their brood (Cam, Ned, and Ruby Jane) was built by Hungarian circus people. Impossible-to-substantiate tales like this one are part of what makes small-town life so charming. (Another part of the appeal: Abita Springs, where the family lives, doesn't have a single traffic light). Even if that tale of the home's heritage is apocryphal, there is something about the nineteenth-century structure that's fanciful—even a little odd. And accordingly, Dave and Michelle have filled the house with their personal treasures, antiques and oddities, and a number of eye-catching, sometimes double-take-inspiring pieces. Many are Dave's creations: he's responsible for a lot of the more straightforward furnishings, a number of the big structural renovations, and other additions, but it's the signs, paintings, and decommissioned movie props that make the biggest statement by far. They're all proof of the strong relationship between beauty and your own hard work. When you do all the decorative heavy lifting yourself, the end result is a home that truly expresses your personal style above all else.

Dave, Michelle, and company relocated from New Orleans in search of relative quiet—and a project. And they found one. The home was in a sad state, with drop ceilings and aluminum siding disguising its most beautiful features, to say nothing of the wear and tear of more than a century. But Dave and Michelle didn't wipe the slate clean with one expansive renovation. Rather, over the course of the last decade and a half, the house's inhabitants have been engaged in a process of making the space into a home.

"We didn't go for a *look*," Michelle explains. "This all just . . . happened." It's true that the resulting house resists easy summary. Architecturally speaking, it's very much an old Louisiana home, and the deep porch and worn wood exterior exude a classic South-

Ruby Jane in the kitchen. There's evidence of Dave's hand in every room in the house—though Michelle half jokingly takes some of the credit for herself. "The kitchen island is just an old dresser from the Goodwill that Dave raised up on legs," she says, adding, "It was my idea!"

ern charm. Inside, though, it's impossible to pinpoint one particular period or influence; rather, the rooms are crowded with a jumbled mix, an accurate reflection of the different tastes, passions, and points of view you're bound to encounter in a family of five. But Dave's is probably the dominant influence. His touch is everywhere. He is an accomplished painter and builder, and he's in the film business, creating sets and props for many major Hollywood productions. Building these pieces is his day job, but bringing them into his home is a decorative choice. They're more than just examples of his handiwork or mementos from favorite jobs; they're big decorative flourishes that imbue the rooms with a charming dose of magic.

The first room you enter via the back of the house is the homey kitchen, which blends sweet period detail with modern touches. The kitchen is as decorated as any other space in the home—a nice reminder that even functional spaces come alive with a few fanciful details. Soft pastel hues and the high ceilings help emphasize the generous light. Dave tore out the badly painted drop ceilings, restoring the

ABOVE In this part of the country, a fair amount of life takes place on the porch—so hanging a painting or bamboo shades to keep the brutal sun at bay, only makes sense. **OPPOSITE** The stove and cabinetry aren't original to the house, though they're in keeping with its spirit—the beautiful bead board, however, is.

room to its original grandeur, but to keep the vibe casual and homey, he and Michelle hung plenty of art on the walls. It's almost impossible to spot the difference between the authentic vintage finds and the props Dave created, and you could argue that it doesn't really matter anyway. Such is the quality of Dave's craftsmanship: it's even near impossible to tell which kitchen cabinetry is antique and which is new; it all serves as the ideal backdrop for the gorgeous vintage stove, a hand-me-down from Michelle's sister. (For the record, the centerpiece cabinet above the stove is new; the wings are vintage cabinets from Michelle's grandmother's house.)

The first thing you notice upon entering the living room is that it's quite similar to the kitchen, with graceful ceilings (their height accentuated by the lovely bead board walls), a pastel color scheme, a mix of art and vintage signs on the walls, lots of light, and a generally laid-back atmosphere. It's a living room meant for *living*. Again, there's plenty of Dave's work on display, both professional and extracurricular. He built the tall bookcases and refitted the old-fashioned ticket booth for a film production. But the home's spaces represent both him and Michelle; the room is finished with pieces that are meaningful to her. The coffee table is a vintage trunk that once belonged to her great-grandmother, an antique touch that tempers the modern statement made by the comfy couch and armchair; and her own collection of

ABOVE Gilded frames and lavish drapes are luxurious touches in the otherwise laid-back living room. The portraits of Creole women are by the couple's friend John Preble. "We mostly collect quirky stuff," Michelle laughs. "I wouldn't call most of it art." **BELOW** Older homes often lack modern conveniences—the Kelseys have no closets to speak of, so armoires provide much-needed storage space. Michelle has been collecting globes for years. **OPPOSITE** It's nearly impossible to distinguish the genuine vintage stuff from the props that have come from Dave's workshop.

vintage globes is on display throughout the room. "My dad ran a vending machine business," Michelle says. "He had machines in Goodwill stores all across New Orleans. We'd tag along and always buy something. I've been collecting globes since high school."

It's possible that the collecting bug is genetic. In Ruby Jane's room, located just off the living room, the young lady of the house is surrounded by an assortment of vintage accessories, once her mother's and now all hers. Her own bags are suspended from the schoolhouse-style coat rack, while pocketbooks suitable for Jackie O. are hung on the wall like fine art. Though this room isn't original to the house—it's an old addition—it is structurally in keeping with the rest of the home (though the door at the head of Ruby Jane's bed now leads nowhere). Here as elsewhere, the vertical bead board draw the eye up to the high ceilings, and Michelle has accentuated the airy feeling by hanging things (vintage handbags, hats, and signs) quite high.

One of the first things Michelle and Dave did upon moving in was to tear out the cheap interior doors and remove the window

Excited by the thought of another little girl (Dave is also dad to Grace Kelsey, featured on page 78), Dave painted this room pink before Ruby Jane was even born. She's inherited her folks' collecting bug—the assortment of vintage bags displayed on the wall once belonged to Michelle.

air-conditioning units. "It's an old house," Michelle says. "It's built for breathing, and there's lots of shade, so even in the heat it's not that bad." Air-conditioning is a modern convenience but hardly a necessity. Doors, on the other hand . . . the family did without these for a while, but eventually did find pieces that complemented the home's overall sensibility. The doors leading to the master bedroom were salvaged from a century-old house just down the street that was destroyed by Hurricane Katrina. The Kelseys' own home was spared, and many friends and neighbors hunkered down there during the storm. The only significant damage the family suffered was the loss of dozens of trees on their property.

The master bedroom has a watery-blue color scheme that establishes a sweetly calming vibe, and decoratively it's a little more restrained than the rest of the home; there's one sign above the door, as opposed to three. Again, here the couple has used the authentically antique and the showbiz approximations: a beaten armoire, with its inset mirrors, used to belong to Michelle's sister, while another storage piece, a chest, was once a movie prop. The point in

ABOVE LEFT Ned, in his room. The vintage pull-down school map is one of many in Michelle's collection. **OPPOSITE** The master bedroom. The room's icy palette helps cool down the space—a visual trick that comes in handy in the middle of a Louisiana summer.

this home is never provenance; Michelle and Dave simply choose to live with what they like, whether it's a century old or something whipped up in Dave's massive workshop. The goal isn't a particular look—it's about keeping things comfortable, and simple. Their everything-goes approach is really summed up by Michelle's occasional inability to recall what's vintage and what's her husband's handiwork, and the fact that collecting, for this family, is instinctive, almost reflexive. "We hardly buy anything," Michelle explains. "Everything just . . . comes here."

ABOVE Odds and ends in Dave's studio, including a long-running game of darts between Dad and his kids. BELOW Ruby Jane in the yard—the whole homestead is a kids' wonderland. OPPOSITE Dave in his workshop. It's nearly impossible to distinguish what he's built from the genuine vintage pieces here and inside the house.

GRAND ILLUSION

JENNIFER CHUSED AND PETER NASHEL, BROOKLYN, NEW YORK

A resourceful New Yorker finds a novel way to get the finer things in life—
and takes a do-it-yourself ethos to new levels of sophistication.

there's irony in the fact that the vast majority of people who truly appreciate superb design are able to do so only from a distance. Real people don't have garden follies or weekend homes in Tunis; real people don't spend six figures on a dining table, or have a Henry Moore on the front lawn. Most design junkies get their fix via magazines and books, and while it's true that Jennifer Chused has spent hours of her life poring over pictures of stately homes, that ultimately wasn't enough. Determined to live the good life, but unable to splurge on it, Jennifer found an audacious compromise: she'd create the good life herself. The Brooklyn apartment she shares with husband, Peter Nashel, and their son, Benjamin, is a stunning and sophisticated home that showcases her impressive abilities—and it challenges most preconceived notions about DIY style.

For Jennifer, finding the apartment was love at first sight. "It's so special," she says. "All the rooms are nicely proportioned. It's so rare to find an apartment in the city that wasn't carved out of a bigger apartment." Located in a 1929 building by the prolific New York–based architect Emery Roth, the apartment has original charm and grace that have survived the decades intact. The rooms are arranged around a central gallery, which serves as both the entryway into the home and the space where Jennifer establishes the decorative tone for the rest of the rooms. It's the home's main artery, so for practical purposes Jennifer has left it relatively unfurnished—with the exception of the long console table. "I wanted to do a statement piece," she explains. "I knew I was never going to find the one I had in my head, so I drew it and had a woodworker build it for me." She was initially reluctant to design her own piece; she's not an architect, after all, or an expert—she just has a knack for math and an extremely thorough nature.

For this, her first foray into design, she was willing to give some leeway to the woodworker

Jennifer and Benjamin in the apartment's central gallery. On the far wall is a vintage shooting range target. Jennifer and Peter's art collection includes everything from a snapshot taken from an airplane window to pages torn from an old book. Art is whatever you want it to be, and even the humblest thing can be suitable for framing.

who executed her plan. He built the console a little taller and a little longer—and all wrong. "I ended up cutting the legs down," she says. "And after that, I learned to just trust my instincts." The resulting piece serves as a visual anchor for the room, a shallow surface on which to display art and framed photos or to toss keys as you come inside. The pale wood helps accentuate the light in the windowless interior room—as does the mirror that hangs above, another piece Jennifer had made to precisely her specifications, including the faux distressing.

In the sun-filled living room, Jennifer wanted to create a space that was comfortable enough for family life but gracious enough for elegant entertaining. "I just can't afford the stuff I want," she confesses. "So I find a way to make it myself." The bookcases in this room were her design, with ample shelving to show off treasures—an array of natural history curiosities, inexpensive art, and other finds. The modern sofa by Ochre has a nice counterpart in the iconic Adolf Loos chair and ottoman, but the furniture is otherwise understated, almost simple. "My favorite part of decorating is fabrics and textures, paints and colors," Jennifer says. "I think that's what really makes the room." The lush textures of the Tibetan rug underfoot make this a comfortable space to sprawl on the floor, and the pale blue walls are just modern enough to update the flea market accessories on display everywhere, from the deer head andirons in the fireplace to the taxidermy

In the living room, Jennifer uses modern furniture but still does justice to the home's elegant old-world vibe. The coffee table from Oly Studio and the armchair, a reproduction of the iconic Adolf Loos design, form an unlikely duo; the couches from Ochre coordinate beautifully (if not surprisingly) with the ornate fireplace.

bird, found at a flea market in Paris. Though some of what's here certainly qualifies as antique—such as the pair of eighteenth-century leather-clad benches underneath the console table—this isn't a room that feels lifeless, or intimidating, as so many fancy rooms can.

The dining room was designed for formality, and accordingly, the centerpiece is a stunning nine-foot-long table. It's set with antique billiard chairs, but again, Jennifer's interest in texture and detail came into play. She had the chairs upholstered in navy patent leather—not the hard, shiny stuff you find on shoes and handbags, but true patent leather, which is incredibly soft and crinkles under the slightest touch. The long table demanded a big light fixture, but the chandelier overhead is glass, and thus doesn't overwhelm diners. The 1930s-era sideboard, found at the vintage shoppers' mecca of Brimfield, is a modern touch that balances out the antique table. Inside, Jennifer discovered a forgotten photograph of an unknown woman. "I love that used pieces have this history that predates me," she says. "That makes them feel so much more special." The dining room opens into the kitchen, a predominantly functional space. The gleaming white tile and glass-front cabinets have a timeless charm—the room is efficient and perfect for modern life, but grand enough that you can almost imagine a butler navigating the narrow passage, ready to serve guests gathered around the table.

ABOVE Built-in bookcases house the library and display Jennifer and Peter's many collections. **OPPOSITE** This console table was originally part of the piece in the foyer. By happy accident, the antique stools, found in Paris, fit perfectly beneath it. The tallest piece in the grouping of vases isn't a vase at all—it's an old cardboard roll, used to hold wallpaper, that Jennifer found on the street.

art isn't quite what it seems. The piece hanging between the two windows in the bedroom is nothing more than a photograph Jennifer took of some handpainted wallpaper she spotted in an old upstate hunting club.

Jennifer displays her most fun-loving and inventive side in Benjamin's playroom. She rescued the overhead light fixture from her in-laws' basement (it was boxed up and destined for the Salvation Army) and used a very pale blue on the walls, putting her own spin on the common and not altogether inspiring convention of painting little boys' rooms blue and little girls' rooms pink. The room is tastefully but still comfortably appointed, suitable for play but not disconnected from the apartment's grown-up rooms. Again, Jennifer has found art in the everyday— the dozen colorful airplanes on the wall are lithographs torn from a volume found in a used-book store.

Though the house would pass muster in any interiors magazine, Jennifer attained its sense of grace and sophistication on her own terms: simply making what she couldn't afford and layering in all manner of unusual treasures. Though none of the flea market and vintage store finds herein are precious, strictly speaking, they're all invested with meaning, which makes them very valuable indeed. It's the smallest details—the velvet ribbon trim on the living room curtains, the old photo of one of the Louvre's galleries, the whitewashed wood bench in the gallery—that Jennifer loves the most. "I can go

ABOVE Jennifer was adamant about having a formal dining room, but admits that the family takes the majority of their meals in the kitchen. BELOW A tufted headboard makes a bed so much more inviting. OPPOSITE "I'm all about the subtleties of color," says Jennifer. "I was so deliberate when it came to choosing paint. Every white in every room is different, every gray is different. It took a lot of time and research—I painted swatches on the wall and would live with them for weeks."

around the apartment and remember the story behind everything," she says. "I can remember all these details about when I bought it, where I was. That's what makes my things so meaningful." It's not the pieces' actual heritage that makes them important; it's how they fit into the story of the family's life. A photo hanging in the foyer is emblematic of Jennifer's whole approach to decorating: it's a simple snapshot taken, by Peter, out of the window of an airplane. It's an unremarkable view but an intriguing image. Most important, it's invested with memories, with a sense of personality. Theirs looks like just another picture-perfect house, and it is—but it's also so much more.

ABOVE Benjamin and Peter at play. Even rooms devoted to play deserve to be decorated seriously. Inside Benjamin's playroom, there's a daybed suitable for grownups, balanced out by a kid-friendly rug by DwellStudio. **OPPOSITE** The planes were torn from an old book and mounted in IKEA frames; they add interest to the walls, but they're still whimsical and appropriately little-boy-ish.

THE ENVIRONMENTALISTS

$t$hese days there's nothing all that new or surprising about green living, but that's not how we're using the term *environmentalist* here. These three homes embrace their environment in a very literal way, using their surroundings—whether it's the great outdoors or iconic twentieth-century architecture—to dictate their décor. The result is a seamless and organic sense of chic that anyone can achieve simply by being attuned to their surroundings.

Outside and inside blend in Lauren Ehrenfeld's Los Angeles house.

INSIDE AND OUT

LAUREN EHRENFELD, LOS ANGELES, CALIFORNIA

This seemingly unremarkable suburban Los Angeles abode is lovingly designed to celebrate the brilliant Southern California climate.

taking an educated guess, Lauren Ehrenfeld figures that her house was built in 1981. It seems like a reasonable estimate—the eighties gave us many wonderful things, but one of that decade's more unfortunately lasting legacies is some pretty ho-hum architecture. Still, it is possible to find the beauty in the everyday, and in Venice, California, there's plenty of natural beauty to go around. So when Lauren began the process of decorating, it was much more about what they stripped away than what she added in, all the better to show to great advantage the relationship between her home and its environs.

That environment is lushly planted and generously sunny. After all, one of the unmistakable advantages of life in Southern California is the temperate climate. This is one of the only places in the country where it's possible—indeed, practical— to live an indoor/outdoor life. And that's very much what Lauren has created here, with a unique perspective and a subtle approach that make the home very much her own. Even the exterior concrete walls refer back to the home's interiors, establishing what awaits guests within: coolly minimal spaces, elemental textures, and much evidence of the natural world.

The house's layout was never altogether complicated—it's a classic suburban home at heart—but still, the first thing Lauren did was strip away. "The house was not very special," Lauren says. "But I saw its potential." Her instinct was dead-on. She added generously proportioned sliding doors to the front of the house, effectively erasing the border between inside and out. This bold step, in conjunction with the comparatively simple act of tearing out the flat ceilings (installing cables to support the structure's walls), totally transformed the home's interior. The main living area—a seamless blend of kitchen and living and dining rooms—feels as light as the garden just outside, while the clean geometry of the exposed beams and the cables

Inside the stripped-down bedroom, the arrangement is surprisingly elegant—a simple bed, a modern bench, and a pair of Matisse linocuts. Here and in the rest of the home, the emphasis is on light, air, and clean, uncluttered spaces.

The cables and beams are a necessity—they're holding the house up, after all—but still quite beautiful. The eye naturally gravitates toward the view outside. "We keep the doors open all day long," says Lauren.

that span the room adds a subtle bit of visual play into a space that's otherwise quite minimal in its décor.

Lauren emphasized the sense of light in the stripped-down (but still nicely functional) kitchen. Open shelving is an airy, unobtrusive alternative to enclosed cabinetry—though recommended only for the truly organized—and offers Lauren a very visible spot to display her collection of Heath ceramics. In addition to being sturdy, the poured-concrete countertops are a decorative touch, referring back to the home's fireplace and the wall around the property's perimeter. The room's cool minimalism celebrates the many elemental textures—the expanses of concrete, the wooden floors, the cabinetry, the beams overhead, and the dining table, which is a very simple, wood plank table. "I saw it in someone's front yard, with paint cans on it, while the owners were renovating," Lauren recounts. "I swapped my old barbeque for it."

Though it's wedged between the open kitchen and the garden just outside, the dining area still feels very much like its own space. It's a reminder that even small spaces can come

ABOVE Lauren opted for open shelving in the kitchen—the better to show off her collection of Heath Ceramics.
OPPOSITE The bedroom is so stripped down that the exposed chimney feels almost ornamental. The bronze elephants were a gift from Lauren's father, who collected East Indian art.

alive with some big furniture—it's so much more chic than trying to cheat the eye with smaller pieces. The décor is simple, in keeping with the family's taste, and the space is further defined by the clean symmetry of the two paintings on the wall and the two pendant lamps overhead.

The living room is defined by a similar statement piece: a deep sofa, perfect for curling up on, set across from a concrete fireplace with a lovely patina of soot. The open plan and eighties architecture ensure that the classically modern lines of the nearby chair (and matching ottoman) and floor lamp blend into the room seamlessly. The bright chrome and angled lines make for an unexpectedly cool complement to the natural textures of what's on display just beyond—the ceramics, the busts, the old books, a few logs for the fire.

As Lauren had already largely erased the divisions between indoors and out, it's not surprising that she decorated the outdoor space as thoughtfully as she did the living room. "The garden was empty except for two birch trees," Lauren recalls. That's certainly no longer the case. She removed one of the original trees to plant the wall of timber bamboo, which, along with the high fences and now-mature trees, ensures privacy from the neighboring apartment building. Thus she can entertain alfresco, or daughter Quinn can lounge on her own, no-dogs-allowed patch of yard, while enjoying the same measure of privacy

BELOW The chair, ottoman, and lamp were all found at flea markets. Lauren clearly favors simple, elemental textures, but she's not aiming for perfection—the soot-stained fireplace has a beauty all its own. **OPPOSITE** The paintings are by Phil Rosenfeld, a friend of Lauren's mother; they depict the Marin Headlands and the Golden Gate Bridge.

The garden is informed by the same minimal sensibility that predominates inside. There's an intimate dining table, a pair of bright butterfly chairs, and little else, besides nature.

they'd get inside the house. The décor is simple but more than just functional—the textures of wood and concrete predominate here as inside, subtly reinforcing the notion that the great outdoors is just another part of the house.

Outside as in, there's evidence of Lauren's precision and confidence. Her career as a stylist has no doubt informed her approach to decorating; she's created a home using relatively few elements, but each is carefully considered.

Lauren's bedroom is even more understated than the main living area. As in the dining room, the arrangement is symmetrical, a nod to elegance in an otherwise informal room. The bedroom is so sparely decorated that its individual elements, though subtle, feel very present. The walls are unpainted—clad only in exterior plaster— while the beams overhead find a natural complement in the flawed floors. "I loved all the knots and holes in the walnut floors," Lauren says. "I asked the installers not to repair any of them." She more than embraced the imperfections—they're precisely what makes the wood beautiful to her. After all, nature's perfection is different from manmade perfection, and this is a home designed to celebrate its environment.

ABOVE The music tree—a homespun alternative to wind chimes. BELOW Quinn at play in her private area of the garden. OPPOSITE The house, as seen from the street.

SHORE THING

**HARRIET MAXWELL MACDONALD AND ANDREW CORRIE,
SHELTER ISLAND, NEW YORK**

The essential element in a beach house is found outside, not in—so the owners of this simple cottage took their cue from Mother Nature.

With the possible exception of movie stars in Malibu and venture capitalists in East Hampton, what most people want out of their beach house is something casual and laid-back, a homey place to unwind on the weekend. There's a nice harmony between the prototypical shingled beach house and the sea, surf, and of course driftwood. Architecture is often informed by context, and the Shelter Island getaway shared by Harriet Maxwell Macdonald; her husband, Andrew Corrie; and their son, Ivo, is evidence that perhaps decorating should be, too.

Interiors are the family business—Harriet is a partner in Ochre, a London-based design collection known for their signature modern furniture and lighting, and she and Andrew oversee the label's retail outlet in New York City—but this house is meant to be a retreat from work life. Thus the home isn't about flawless design. It's incredibly chic, but you might not initially take it for the home of someone in the design business, which is just how the couple wanted it. "I didn't want everything to look squeaky-clean and brand-new," Harriet explains. "We spend a lot of time out here, and I wanted it to feel informal and comfortable." And so it does. Via décor that emphasizes the same natural colors and materials, shapes and textures, that surround the house, Harriet and Andrew have created a serene space where the family and their guests can truly relax—and isn't that the whole point of a beach house?

Visitors enter right into the tiny home's nerve center: a combination of foyer, living room, dining room, and kitchen. The way these zones spill into one another is very much in the idiom of late 1970s architecture, of which the house is a prime example, and the semi-open plan helps reinforce the easygoing vibe Harriet and Andrew were after.

Harriet and Andrew favor modern furniture, and have managed to strike the balance between cool, contemporary lines and good old-fashioned comfort, pairing overstuffed couches with a minimal coffee table and spindly dining chairs with a weathered old credenza. The antique ottoman beside the couch, which once belonged to Harriet's grandmother, has been updated in a simple, neutral Nubuck.

This isn't a house about formal luncheons at the table or after-dinner drinks in the library—it's design for real life, with plenty of places to lounge. The banister that divides the passage downstairs from the main living space creates an entryway of sorts into the home. It's lined with rocks the family found on the beach, a subtle, almost accidental design gesture. It's a motif that recurs elsewhere, and that simple juxtaposition of wood and stone strikes the perfect note in a cozy beach cottage.

Given their line of work, the couple has easy access to a beautiful selection of furniture and lighting. But the sophistication and polish for which their designs are known aren't necessarily well suited to how they'd envisioned life at the beach. "A lot of the furniture we design is more suited to the urban home," Harriet says. "Chandeliers aren't really appropriate for a beach house." Elements from their collection

ABOVE Stones, collected along the shore, are a natural complement to the woodsy interior. OPPOSITE The cabinet, found at the Brimfield Antiques Show, is topped with a sculptural lamp by Ochre. FOLLOWING PAGES: LEFT Not crazy about the color of the tiles behind the fireplace, Harriet applied the same finish there as on the rest of the walls. "I was aiming to soften the whole room, make it feel more like a beach house," Harriet says. "So I washed over the tile too. I didn't think it would hold but it did nicely, and took the color down just a notch." RIGHT The tiny kitchen is one thing the owners hope to renovate. "It's quite a nice kitchen to cook in," Harriet says. "There's a lovely view, and everything is close together and very reachable. But the minute there are people in the house it starts to feel very claustrophobic!" The rough-hewn cabinetry has its utilitarian charms, though, and Harriet has added a dose of whimsy by using ribbon to Ivo-proof the lower cabinets.

have nonetheless found their way into the house, and while the long sofa or the inviting round ottoman wouldn't be out of place in an Upper East Side town house, it's equally at home here, mostly because Harriet's paired such grand silhouettes with rocks found on the beach instead of gilt-frame oil paintings. It's possible to use context to change the vibe of a given piece; even a chandelier can work in an informal room, much as a humble store-bought mass-produced item can fit right into even the most opulent environment.

The generous sofa is offset nicely by the coffee table: both are long, but while the couch is overstuffed, the table is spindly; the former is upholstered right down to the floor, while the latter seems to float just above it. Though Harriet and Andrew didn't bother with a big renovation, initially the house wasn't necessarily move-in ready. "The walls were so orange and gloomy," Harriet recalls. "It was a bit like a Swiss chalet." A ski lodge was precisely the opposite of what they were after, so Harriet sanded the color off the walls, applying a bright new wash to finish them. The lighter walls—in conjunction with the many windows and the

ABOVE Long, horizontal lines create the illusion that the living room is bigger than it is. The emphasis on neutrals further helps a smallish room feel airy and light. OPPOSITE Harriet purchased the painting from a student at London's Royal College of Art. The simple forms echo the stones she's scattered casually throughout the house.

sliding glass doors—flood the space with ample light and imbue it with a distinctly beachy vibe.

Even in the lighter finish, the walls have a very strong, woody presence. Accordingly, the couple layered in lots of clean whites to balance that out. The white-washed ceiling, neutral upholstery, and myriad white accessories, including the stones, help bring more light into the room. The fluffy rug—made of six sheepskins—adds lavish texture that's a nice contrast to all the wood.

ABOVE Harriet, and the home's stunning view. BELOW Harriet's home office. OPPOSITE Downstairs, lush textures—from the rumpled couch to the curtains that pool onto the floor—provide a soft, inviting counterpoint to all that wood.

239

The family's private rooms continue in this natural, beach-inspired vein. They are stripped-down and laid-back, designed for comfort above all else. In the master bedroom there's little more than the bed, dressed in simple white. The beaten Bertoia chair provides a refreshingly modern contrast to the cottage-y interior, as do the acrylic nightstands. The slate blue walls establish a sense of serenity. "I've done most of my bedrooms that color," Harriet says. "It's very calming." It's an effect that's underscored by the lack of visual clutter within.

Ivo's room was treated similarly, perhaps counterintuitively. Most children's rooms burst with color and clutter, but his is a quiet, understated space. "Andrew had decided that this was going to be his study," Harriet says. "So I had to move all of his rubbish out. The room just evolved from there." She simply added the Amish crib, an old armchair that had belonged to her husband, and a couple of whimsical mobiles. "The room had that nice shelf in it anyway," Harriet adds, summing up her approach to design not just in the nursery but in the house as a whole. "It's a nice room that's not really decorated. It didn't really need it."

ABOVE AND OPPOSITE Children's rooms don't have to be all primary colors and cartoon characters; Ivo's room is as chic and minimal as the rest of the house. Instead of a rocking chair, Harriet used a comfy old armchair of Andrew's.

THOROUGHLY MODERN

STEPHANIE LOCKEMANN, CHICAGO, ILLINOIS

This big-city apartment in the sky has an understated interior designed as an homage to its exuberant exterior.

It might seem only natural that Stephanie Lockemann would take up residence in Marina City. She's an architect, and the reinforced concrete towers are perhaps some of the most distinctive architecture in the city of Chicago. But Stephanie's interest in the space wasn't professional. While hunting for an apartment, she consulted a psychic, who advised her to find a place on the water. Stephanie reasoned that the psychic was referring to Marina City (or the Corncob Towers, as the fanciful structures are commonly called). She visited the complex and did indeed fall in love. Inside her tiny five-hundred-square-foot studio, Stephanie has created a quiet space with all the creature comforts of home, and she did so in a way that's a subtle homage to a building that's as iconic as it is iconoclastic.

The concrete structure was designed to last through the ages; the interiors were not, but part of what makes Stephanie's apartment so special is that it bears so many traces of its 1960s provenance, from the sliding wood screen between the main space and the kitchen to the glass mosaic tile in the bathroom. Even without these little details, the sense of place is inescapable, as it dictates the apartment's unusual (some might say impossible) floor plan. The apartment, like all units in the building, is a wedge shape, tapered at the entrance and then opening up toward the great big balcony. Or think of it like this: the apartment is shaped like an ice cream cone, the balcony is the scoop atop it. In decorating the space, Stephanie faced not only that challenge but also the hurdle of making the studio apartment feel like a sophisticated and grown-up home.

The iconic Marina City towers are an instantly recognizable part of the Chicago skyline. High-rise living generally means sacrificing outdoor space, but one of the most appealing things about life in this particular complex is each unit's deep, private terrace.

Since this was Stephanie's first real place of her own—she'd lived with room-mates before—she decided to start from scratch, choosing furniture and other pieces specifically with the apartment in mind. As it's a small space, this wasn't prohibitively expensive. To make it even easier on her bottom line, Stephanie relied largely on junk shop finds and her own two hands for the pieces to breathe new life into the 1960s-era space.

There's no bedroom, but Stephanie hasn't skimped on her own comfort in the least. "I didn't want to sacrifice having a bedroom just because it's a studio," she says. "Rather than try to hide my bed away, I decided to just celebrate the fact that this is a studio." She did so with a bed grand enough for a hotel. She made the upholstered headboard herself—with plywood, batting, and textured fabric in a simple putty color. Given the space constraints, every piece besides the bed must pull double duty: the console table is at once nightstand, desk, and a place for guests to set down their drinks. Stephanie had a working sketch of the table of her dreams, the one that could fulfill all these functions. "Then, just like magic, I found it," she says.

ABOVE The apartment is a time capsule of midcentury design: the original fixtures remain in the kitchen, bath, and elsewhere. OPPOSITE Glass furniture is ideal for small spaces—the table is utterly functional, but disappears nicely. The armchair's white upholstery similarly fades into the background.

The junk store discovery was painted gold, but she spray-painted it white, totally transforming it. Beneath it, a duo of upholstered stools—also bought secondhand; they were pink when Stephanie found them—in an inviting gray velvet stand at the ready for guests.

Lacking walls, Stephanie used the white rug to help distinguish living from sleeping area. The simple rug's crisp white pops against the apartment's unremarkable tan carpeting and the black coffee table above it. "I like simple furniture," Stephanie says, "and midcentury furniture tends to be really minimalist, which is why I've ended up with a few pieces from that era. I'm just not that interested in the iconic styles that everybody seems to have." Though it's not one of that special handful of immediately recognizable modern styles, the coffee table does have an unmistakable midcentury provenance that nicely suits the apartment's overall vibe. The long couch has a similar feel. It, too, was a junk store buy, and as such, a gamble. "The couch is a classic shape, and it was dirt cheap," Stephanie says. Thus, it was just right. "I pulled all the covers off and threw them in the washing machine. I was worried it

ABOVE Stephanie has focused on acquiring pieces that can serve multiple functions—key in a studio space such as this. OPPOSITE She's short on wall space, so Stephanie opted for lavish bedding to add a bit more visual interest to the room. She made the upholstered headboard herself.

would fall apart." Beyond aesthetics, that's part of the appeal of midcentury design; it was built to last. It's hard to imagine a department store sofa purchased today surviving four decades from now.

"I'm a completely intuitive decorator," Stephanie says. "The apartment is so easy—a neutral palette, with tiny splashes of color. You can get different pillows, flowers, bedding, candles, whatever. But what anchors the room, what stays, is the neutrals." The white wingback armchair is a prime example of that. Stephanie had the chair, found secondhand, upholstered in an outdoor-grade fabric hardy enough to withstand red wine stains. It's paired with a glass table with a quintessentially 1970s vibe, but the combination is unexpectedly chic. As a foil to all this white, Stephanie did indulge in one big colorful wall— it's a muted gray, but in the pristine space, it's very vibrant and present. An assortment of antique mounted antlers hangs above the couch, a nod not to the apartment's midcentury heritage but to Stephanie's own upbringing: the antlers once hung in her parents' home in Germany. All more than a century old, they're a surprising flourish in this most modern of interiors, a quirky addition that brings personality into the room and keeps it from feeling like an attempt to re-create a period space.

ABOVE Bedside curiosities mix with functional pieces. BELOW Since Stephanie's birthday is in the winter months, she can't celebrate it with an indoor/outdoor party. Instead, she's got an annual tradition of celebrating the birth of Bertrand Goldberg, Marina City's innovative architect. "This building is so special," she says. "It was the tallest building ever built with reinforced concrete—the engineering is amazing." She hangs the tiny snapshot of Goldberg with a model of his famous project on the front door when she's celebrating his birthday. OPPOSITE Texture can add real depth in a minimal color scheme. The fuzzy pillows, undulating porcelain plate, and nubby rug underfoot bring a bit of warmth into the cool room.

The massive balcony is one of the apartment's most unique features. "These balconies are almost one hundred and seventy-five square feet," Stephanie says. "It's so rare to have that much space outside, especially on the twenty-ninth floor." Weather permitting, she uses her exterior space as much as possible, for herself and to entertain guests. She dressed up the workaday outdoor furniture with eye-catching pillows in an outdoor fabric by Trina Turk. "I would never [normally] put such a signature upholstery on furniture," Stephanie says, "but you can always switch out pillows." For the whole studio, Stephanie aimed for an inviting space that felt like a boutique hotel, and here the bright fabric and jet-age furniture on top of the layer of Astroturf make the outdoor space feel almost like a little slice of Palm Springs in Chicago.

"I'm an architect, but it's completely unglamorous," Stephanie says of her home. "A typical workday is about permits and compliances. Decorating is my outlet."

"When I first moved in, I'd set my alarm for 5:30," Stephanie recalls with a laugh, "just so I could have a cup of coffee on the balcony before work." The sensibility of her outdoor décor brings a touch of Palm Springs to the Windy City.

RESOURCES

As we put this book together, I found myself in home after home asking the same question: Where did you get that? The homes in these pages are so wildly distinct that it was a surprise to hear so many residents cite the same stores, websites, and markets as their go-to resources. Here are our subjects' secret suppliers—and a few of my own most trusted sources. Happy hunting!

One-Stop Shopping

TARGET www.target.com

IKEA www.ikea.com

EBAY www.ebay.com

WEST ELM www.westelm.com

URBAN OUTFITTERS www.urbanoutfitters.com

ANTHROPOLOGIE www.anthropologie.com

CONTAINER STORE www.containerstore.com

DWR www.dwr.com

CRATE&BARREL www.crateandbarrel.com

CB2 www.cb2.com

RESTORATION HARDWARE www.restorationhardware.com

WILLIAMS SONOMA HOME www.wshome.com

MY DECO www.mydeco.com

CONRAN SHOP www.conranusa.com

DESIGN PUBLIC www.designpublic.com

LAYLA GRACE www.laylagrace.com

AMAZON www.amazon.com

Building/Renovating

LOWES www.lowes.com

HOME DEPOT www.homedepot.com

YOURCHITECT www.yourchitect.com

REMODELISTA www.remodelista.com

GREEN DEPOT www.greendepot.com

Paint

BENJAMIN MOORE www.benjaminmoore.com

FARROW & BALL www.farrowandball.com

YOLO COLORHOUSE www.yolocolorhouse.com

Wallpaper

GRAHAM & BROWN www.grahambrown.com

TIMOROUROUS BEASTIES www.timorousbeasties.com

OSBORNE AND LITTLE www.osborneandlittle.com

COLE AND SONS www.coleandsons.com

CAVERN HOME www.cavernhome.com

Flooring

LUMBER LIQUIDATORS www.lumberliquidators.com

SIMPLE FLOORS www.simplefloors.com

SHAW www.shawfloors.com

MOHAWK www.mowhakflooring.com

Rugs

MADELINE WEINRIB www.madelineweinrib.com

FLOR www.flor.com

ANGELA ADAMS www.angelaadams.com

EMMA GARDNER www.emmagardnerdesign.com

COMPANY C www.companyc.com

MERIDA MERIDIAN www.meridameridian.com

THE RUG COMPANY www.therugcompany.com

DASH & ALBERT www.dashandalbert.com

Fabric

ROBERT ALLEN www.robertallendesign.com

REPRO DEPOT www.reprodepot.com

JOANN'S www.joann.com

CALICO CORNERS www.calicocorners.com

Furniture

OLY STUDIO www.olystudio.com

WHITE FURNITURE www.whiteonwhite.com

BLU DOT www.bludot.com

OCHRE www.ochrestore.com

ROOM & BOARD www.roomandboard.com

MITCHELL GOLD + BOB WILLIAMS www.mgbw.com

BDDW www.bddw.com

JAYSON HOME & GARDEN www.jaysonhome.com

KNOLL www.knoll.com

BOBO INTRIGUING OBJECTS www.bobointriguingobjects.com

JONATHAN ADLER www.jonathanadler.com

Bedding

DWELLSTUDIO www.dwellstudio.com

AREA www.areahome.com

THE COMPANY STORE www.thecompanystore.com

FRETTE www.frette.com

GARNET HILL www.garnethill.com

MATTEO www.matteohome.com

OLATZ www.olatz.com

JOHN ROBSHAW www.johrobshaw.com

Lighting

CIRCA LIGHTING www.circalighting.com

Y LIGHTING www.ylighting.com

OLAMPIA www.olampia.com

NOVA68 www.nova68.com

Accessories

CANVAS www.shopcanvashomestore.com

GLOBAL TABLE www.globaltable.com

VELOCITY ART AND DESIGN www.velocityartanddesign.com

TED MEUHLING www.tedmeuhling.com

COMERFORD HENNESSY www.comerfordhennessy.com

GUMPS www.gumps.com

MOMA STORE www.momastore.org

TREILLAGE www.treillageonline.com

PERCH www.perch-home.com

VITRA www.vitra.com

CALYPSO HOME www.calypso-celle.com

3 POTATO 4 www.threepotatofourshop.com

GRAHAM & BROWN www.grahambrown.com

ARTNET.COM www.artnet.com

NATURAL CURIOSITIES www.naturalcuriosities.com

THOMAS PAUL www.thomaspaul.com

JOHN DERIAN www.johnderian.com

DE VERA www.deveraobjects.com

Kids' Stuff

GIGGLE www.giggle.com

GENIUS JONES www.geniusjones.com

NETTO COLLECTION www.nettocollection.com

OEUF www.oeufnyc.com

Q COLLECTION www.qcollection.com

DWELLSTUDIO www.dwellstudio.com

SERENA & LILY www.serenaandlily.com

STOKKE www.stokke.com

Antique/Vintage

GOODWILL www.shopgoodwill.com

EBAY www.ebay.com

1STDIBS www.1stdibs.com

CIRCA 50 www.circa50.com

HOUSING WORKS www.housingworks.org

V & M www.vandm.com

WRIGHT www.wright20.com

SOLLO RAGO www.ragoarts.com

LOST CITY ARTS www.lostcityarts.com

LAS VENUS www.lasvenus.com

WYETH www.wyethhome.com

DUANE MODERN www.duanemodern.com

RUBY LANE www.rubylane.com

Flea Markets

BRIMFIELD ANTIQUES AND FLEA MARKET SHOW
www.brimfield.com

ROSE BOWL FLEA MARKET www.rgcshows.com

THE SABLON ANTIQUES MARKET
Sablon Square, Brussels, Belgium

CLINGANCOURT
Marche aux Puces de Saint-Ouen
140 Rue des Rosiers
93400 Saint Ouen, FRANCE
01 40 12 32 58

MULFORD FARM ANTIQUES SHOW
10 James Lane
East Hampton, NY 11937
Phone: 631-324-6850

FIRST MONDAY TRADE DAYS
290 East Dyler St
Canton, TX 75103

STORMVILLE AIRPORT FLEA MARKET
www.stormvilleairportfleamarket.com

ACKNOWLEDGMENTS

I would like to thank all of the people who made this book possible. To Melanie Acevedo—for making my concepts look better than I could have imagined, for traveling all over the country with me on this crazy journey, and for becoming one of my best friends in the process. I am also so grateful to Rumaan Alam for writing this with me. Rumaan—you make my words funnier, better, and clearer than I ever could. Thank you for getting the concept so thoroughly and making sense of a somewhat nebulous idea. To Molly Peterson, producer, and so much more. You got us across the country and back and made friends with everyone on the way. You inspire me constantly with your innate ability to connect with everyone you meet. And to the rest of our traveling band—Beau States, Sophie Von Hahn, Brian Delaney, and Christopher Davis: thanks so much for being part of the Dwellabration.

I would also like to thank the team at Clarkson Potter and all the amazing people who touched *Undecorate.* To Doris Cooper for giving me the chance; to Judy Pray for getting me started; and to my amazing editor, Rosy Ngo, for taking a whole bunch of ideas and shaping them into something real. Your vision gave this book its purpose.

I would also like to thank the team at DwellStudio, past and present. The inspiration for this book came from the amazing people I work with every day.

I have to thank all of the subjects of *Undecorate* for letting us into their homes, families, and hearts: Lisa Borgnes Giramonti, Piero and Luca Giramonti; Andy Newcom; Benjamin, Lucy, Oden, and Genifer Goodman Sohr; Valorie Hart and Alberto Paz; Kim Ficaro and James Wilson; Grace Kelsey and Kenyan Lewis; Harry Heissmann and Mark King; Heidi Hough and Art Detrich; Caitlin Wylde; Christina Sacalis and Kurt, Emmett, and Ila Pearl Steinert; Erica Tanov, Steven Emerson, Isabelle Ruby Tanov, and Hugo Emerson Tanov; Chase Booth and Gray Davis; Natascha Couvreur and Olivier, Kaya, Marlo, and Nel Azancot; Michelle, Dave, Cam, Ned, and Ruby Kelsey; Jennifer Chused and Peter and Benjamin Nashel; Lauren Ehrenfeld and Quinn De Souza; Harriet Maxwell Macdonald and Andrew and Ivo Corrie; and Stephanie Lockemann. You all welcomed us in, were such gracious hosts, and gave us access to your lives. I celebrate your style and wish we could visit each one of you every summer.

My deepest thanks to my husband, Joshua—for inspiring me, for being my partner at work and in life, and for holding down the fort while I worked on *Undecorate.* And to Isabelle and William—you both are my greatest design triumph. I can't imagine anything more perfect than the two of you.

INDEX